T H E Industrial Revolution
for KIDS

**The People and Technology
That Changed the World**

WITH 21 ACTIVITIES

C H E R Y L   M U L L E N B A C H

CHICAGO
REVIEW
PRESS

For Duke and Lori
"The Girls" Kim, Lindy, Cindy, and Dixie
And always for Richard L. Wohlgamuth

For educator resources and more, please visit
www.cherylmullenbachink.com

© 2014 by Cheryl Mullenbach
All rights reserved
First edition
Published by Chicago Review Press, Incorporated
814 North Franklin Street
Chicago, Illinois 60610
ISBN 978-1-61374-690-5

Library of Congress Cataloging-in-Publication Data
Mullenbach, Cheryl.
    The industrial revolution for kids : the people
and technology that changed the world : with
21 activities / Cheryl Mullenbach. — First edition.
        pages cm. — (For kids series)
    Includes bibliographical references and index.
    ISBN 978-1-61374-690-5 (paperback)
    1. Industrial revolution—United States—Juvenile
literature. 2. Industries—United States—
History—Juvenile literature. 3. Technological
innovations—Economic aspects—United States—
History—Juvenile literature. 4. Capitalists and
financiers—United States—Juvenile literature.
5. Businesspeople—United States—Juvenile
literature. I. Title.
    HC105.M85 2014
    330.973′08—dc23
                    2014016755

Cover and interior design: Monica Baziuk
Cover images: (front, clockwise from upper right)
vintage hand sewing machine, Shutterstock/
Againstar; roller skater, courtesy of the Library
of Congress, Prints & Photographs Division, LC-
USZ62-55467; workers building the Boonsborough
Turnpike Road, courtesy of the Federal Highway
Administration, US Department of Transportation;
skyscrapers, courtesy of the Library of Congress,
Prints & Photographs Division, Detroit Publishing
Company Collection, LC-D4-13088; newsgirls in
Delaware, 1910, courtesy of the Library of Congress,
Prints & Photographs Division, LC-USZ62-75164;
train car, Courtesy of the Library of Congress, Prints
& Photographs Division, LC-DIG-ggbain-04545;
(back, clockwise from upper right) young radish
seller in Cincinnati, Ohio, courtesy of the Library of
Congress, Prints & Photographs Division, National
Child Labor Committee Collection, LC-DIG-
nclc-03199; early Ford car, courtesy of the Library
of Congress, Prints & Photographs Division,
LC-USZ62-21222
Interior illustrations: Jim Spence

Printed in the United States of America
5   4

CONTENTS

ACKNOWLEDGMENTS

THANKS TO MY EDITOR, Lisa Reardon, at Chicago Review Press. Also, thanks to Christina Stern for her professional insights. Special gratitude to the Miller family—Jeff, Kristie, Bailey, Zack, and Brooklyn—for their expertise and contributions to the project. Bailey's input and unique perspective was invaluable. Zack's fascination with the boy miner photos was an inspiration. And Brooklyn's help in papermaking was priceless.

TIME LINE

1873   Economic depression
(Panic of 1873) hits

1876   Alexander Graham Bell patents the
telephone; American Centennial
Exhibition is held in Philadelphia

1877   Nez Perce Chief Joseph surrenders
to US government; Great
Railroad Strike occurs;
Thomas Edison files a patent
for the phonograph

1879   College football debuts

1880   Thomas Edison develops an
electric lightbulb; John
D. Rockefeller's Standard
Oil owns 90 percent of oil
refineries in the United States

1882   Chinese Exclusion Act is passed

1884   First skyscraper is built in Chicago

1886   American Federation of Labor
forms; Haymarket Riot occurs

1889   Jane Addams establishes
Hull House

1891   James Naismith invents the
game of basketball

1892   Carnegie Steel Company is
the largest US steel maker;
Homestead Strike occurs

1893   Economic depression (Panic
of 1893) hits; Chicago hosts
the World's Columbian
Exposition; Illinois governor
pardons surviving Haymarket
Riot participants

1894   Pullman Strike occurs

1897   Nation's first subway is
completed in Boston

1899   First juvenile court system is
established in Illinois; Marshall
Taylor wins the world one-mile
track cycling championship

1901   Pan-American Exposition is
held in Buffalo, New York;
President William McKinley
is assassinated

1903   Wright Brothers complete the first
successful airplane flight

1904   Louisiana Purchase Exposition
is held in St. Louis, Missouri

1905   Bessie Moore becomes the first
woman to win the US Women's
Singles Championship four times

1906   Upton Sinclair shocks readers
with his book *The Jungle*; Pure
Food and Drug Act is enacted

1913   Henry Ford sets up the
first assembly line to
manufacture cars

During the Industrial Revolution children like Lucy Larcom and this young cotton spinner worked long hours in textile mills.

INTRODUCTION

Lucy Larcom, 11-Year-Old Doffer

"**I THOUGHT IT WOULD BE A PLEASURE** to feel that I was not a trouble or burden or expense to anybody... it really was not hard, just to change the bobbins of the spinning frames every three-quarters of an hour or so, with half a dozen other little girls who were doing the same thing."

Lucy Larcom wrote those words about her first day as an 11-year-old mill girl in Lowell, Massachusetts, in 1835. At eight years of age, Lucy had moved with her mother and siblings from Beverly, Massachusetts, when her dad died. Her mother ran a boardinghouse for women who worked at the Lawrence Manufacturing Company.

Lucy's older sisters went to work in the mills, and when the family needed more income, Lucy began her job as a *doffer*. She spent her days changing sewing bobbins on the water-powered looms that spun thread and wove fabric. Sometimes Lucy and the other girls explored the mill or played games among the machinery. Although the work wasn't hard, Lucy did work long hours—5 AM to 7 PM. Lucy's $1 in weekly wages helped the Larcoms keep a roof over their heads and food on their table.

Lucy occasionally took time to gaze out the window at the Merrimack River as it flowed past the mill. In the summer it was difficult for Lucy to stay confined in the mill all day. She wished she had wings so she could fly away from the deafening clang of the machines. She dreamed of becoming a teacher or a writer.

Lucy worked at the mill until she was 22. Then she moved with her married sister from Massachusetts to Illinois. In 1846 that trip was an adventure. The women boarded a steamboat named the *Worchester* in a snowstorm for the first leg of the 1,000-mile journey. There were beds on the boat, but they were three wooden shelves, or *berths*—one on top of the other. Lucy was sandwiched into the middle bed. And what made the situation almost unbearable was that Lucy got terribly seasick. Sharing the cabin with two other seasick family members and a crying baby made for a nasty trip.

At Cumberland, Maryland, Lucy boarded a stagecoach to cross the Allegheny Mountains. Nine passengers and a baby spent the night packed into the tight quarters. Lucy described it as "miserable." They caught another boat named the *Clipper* as they made their way to St. Louis, Missouri. There they spent the night on a canal boat as they waited for repairs to be made to the canal. They passed through the locks during the night—a very slow trip. In the morning they arrived at their destination—Illinois's Looking Glass Prairie.

In Illinois, Lucy was able to fulfill one of her dreams. After attending the Monticello Female Seminary, she took a job as a traveling teacher—spending three months at each school before moving on to the next. She was paid $14 per month but had to pay $1.25 per week for room and board—usually with the family of one of her students.

When Lucy worked as a doffer in the mill, she used to dream of being a teacher. But once she fulfilled her dream, she may have wished she were back at the mill sometimes—especially when she had to deal with unruly students. One day one of her students, a boy she described as a "misbehaving urchin," was acting very badly—annoying the other students. Lucy made the boy sit on a stool away from the other students, near the fireplace. She turned her back on the boy and continued to work with the other children. When she turned to look at the "urchin," the stool was empty! Where was that naughty child? The other children directed Lucy's attention outside where they saw the mischievous boy dancing in front of the school! He had escaped by climbing up the fireplace chimney!

Despite the occasional misbehaving urchin, Lucy loved teaching. She decided to move back to Massachusetts in 1853. She taught at Wheaton Seminary for several years but left to make a living as a writer. She was a very successful writer—publishing several books of poetry and a book about her days as a mill girl.

Lucy Larcom lived during a time that became known as the Industrial Revolution in America. It was a time when extreme—or *revolutionary*—changes occurred in the way people lived and worked. Those changes were a big part of Lucy's life, from her days as a mill girl to her adult years as a teacher and writer. In some ways Lucy was like many other people who lived during the Industrial Revolution. She worked in a factory to help support her family. She struggled to make a living. She dreamed of a better life.

Lucy's dreams became reality. Many of the men, women, and children who lived during the Industrial Revolution were not as lucky as Lucy. Throughout the 1800s and into the 1900s, many spent their lives in factories. They had little or no education. And, unlike Lucy, their dreams of leaving the drudgery of the factory never became real.

The Industrial Revolution spanned about 100 years and introduced revolutionary changes to many parts of American life. Enormous shifts occurred in the way people traveled, communicated, worked, and played. Many of those changes brought about improvements in people's lives. Some created hardship and misery.

When 11-year-old Lucy Larcom walked to work at the mill in 1835, she couldn't have imagined the world that would exist by the time she was old in the 1890s. She may have looked back to the days at the mill and thought about the amazing changes she witnessed over time. When she was an adult, she wrote about her childhood days at the mill: "Life to me, as I looked forward, was a bright blank of mystery."

As you learn about the revolution that rocked the lives of kids growing up during the 1800s, think about your way of life. What would those kids say about the way you travel, communicate, work, and play? Try to imagine the world 100 years from now. What inventions and new ideas can you envision? Maybe they will pave the way for the next revolution.

Lucy Larcom.

Courtesy of the Marion B. Gebbie Archives & Special Collections, Wallace Library, Wheaton College, Norton, MA

A TIME OF SWEEPING CHANGE

THE MARRIAGE OF LOUISA PIERPONT MORGAN, eldest daughter of J. Pierpont (J. P.) Morgan, took place on a November afternoon in 1900 in New York City. J. P. Morgan was one of the wealthiest men in the world. He had made his millions as a banker and business investor. Louisa's dress was fashioned from French lace; her veil was held in place by a large spray of diamonds. The reception was held at the Morgan mansion—the first house in New York City lit entirely by electricity. The bride and groom received over 400 gifts, including paintings, furniture, silver dinnerware, and gold plates. Mr. and Mrs. Morgan gave their daughter a diamond tiara and necklace—and $1 million.

About the same time that Louisa Morgan was celebrating her wedding, Nora Nelson, a young woman who worked at a factory in Troy, New York, was thinking about marriage too. She worked long days for little pay at a factory that manufactured detachable shirt collars. When she heard Tacoma, Washington, was a city with an unusually large number of single men, she got an idea. Nora sent a letter to a Tacoma newspaper writing that there were plenty of single women working at the factory who would be willing to move west for a suitable husband. Within a very short time, she received 250 letters from interested men! Nora decided to form a *matrimonial club* made up of women with marriage in mind who would consider a move to Washington. Everyone who joined paid monthly dues to help send members to Tacoma. Within a day Nora's club had 40 members.

Louisa Morgan and Nora Nelson lived at the same time and only about 150 miles apart, but their lives were vastly different. Nora's situation was much like that of thousands of young people at the time—constant struggle in a harsh, bleak environment. Louisa's circumstances were shared by a privileged few. And though Louisa and Nora never knew one another, they depended on each other for their livelihoods. Nora's job existed because of wealthy investors like J. P. Morgan, and Louisa's lifestyle was possible because of hardworking men and women like Nora.

FORMER TEACHER REVOLUTIONIZES MANUFACTURING

When a former schoolteacher from Connecticut promised government officials in 1798 that he could produce 10,000 muskets within a span of only two years, it seemed like an impossible task. But Eli Whitney convinced the officials that he was up for the challenge, because he had a new way of manufacturing guns. As it turned out, Eli came up a little short on his promise. The actual number of muskets he produced was only 500.

But it didn't seem to matter to the government officials. They were willing to forgive Eli because he told them about his unusual method for making things. His new idea was called *interchangeable parts*. No one knew it at the time, but Eli's ideas would become the basis for a process that would revolutionize manufacturing.

Eli knew that if guns were made using interchangeable parts, they could be made much faster. But for parts to be interchangeable, they had to be exactly alike. And that was possible only if the parts were made by machines—not people.

Eli's method would eventually be applied to many different products. His ideas were used almost 100 years later by Henry Ford, who manufactured automobiles. By using interchangeable parts, Henry was able to mass produce automobiles. Without Eli's innovations, mass production of cars and other products would not have occurred.

Revolutionary Changes in Industries

LOUISA MORGAN and Nora Nelson lived during the time that became known as the Industrial Revolution. It was a time when workers began to use machines, rather than their hands, to make products. The Industrial Revolution occurred between the early 1800s and 1900s in America. Over about 100 years revolutionary changes took place in industries—manufacturing, transportation, and communication.

It's difficult to say how and where these innovations started, because it wasn't just one event or person who brought about the Industrial Revolution. But most historians agree it began with machines designed to make thread and cloth—the textile industry. These inventions led to even more innovations, in areas other than textiles. Soon machines were used for transportation and communication too. This was a shift, because before 1800, people and animals supplied the energy for making, transporting, and communicating things.

These remarkable changes meant people from all backgrounds worked, traveled, and communicated differently than their parents and grandparents had. They played and relaxed in new ways too. It seemed as though every part of life was undergoing gigantic change.

Changes in the Way Products Were Made

FOR CENTURIES workers made products like shoes, clothes, tools, furniture, and food by hand. Skilled craftsmen and craftswomen, not machines, produced these goods. As machines were invented to make these products, people began to work in different ways.

Before the Industrial Revolution, people worked in small shops, on farms, or in their homes. Women made clothes, soap, and candles for the family. Men chopped wood for fuel and raised animals for food. Most of the items they used every day were homemade or purchased from local craftspeople. Many people in America lived in rural areas and small towns.

As the Industrial Revolution began in the 1800s, that began to change gradually. More and more items that people used every day were made in factories in large cities. People operated the machines. Each worker made one part of an item. All the parts were put together for a finished product. It was a very different way of working.

Samuel and Harriet Slater opened a factory in Rhode Island in the late 1700s that made thread—an important product for textile manufacturing, but it was only one part of making cloth. They hired hand weavers in the community to finish the cloth in their homes.

Francis Cabot Lowell took the process a step further in Massachusetts. Like Samuel Slater, Francis used ideas he had seen at a mill in England. In 1813 he formed the Boston Manufacturing Company in Waltham, Massachusetts. He later moved his company to the banks of the Merrimack River at a location that became known as Lowell, Massachusetts. At Francis's mill, machines wove the thread into cloth, and all the other steps in the process were completed within the mill. This was a turning point in the making of cloth. Soon other investors built textile mills in the northeastern states. From 1814 to 1850 many mills were started. This growth of the textile industry marks the beginning of the Industrial Revolution in America.

As the Industrial Revolution evolved between 1800 and the early 1900s, many improvements were made to machines. People were constantly adjusting to new ways of working and making products. Changes in the way people worked meant changes in other parts of their lives.

When Samuel and Harriet Slater built their factory, they liked to hire families. Other factory owners copied the Slaters' idea. They offered work to parents and children. It wasn't unusual for an entire family to move to a factory town and go to work at the same mill. There were special jobs for the children. Some owners provided houses for the families, and some built stores where the workers could purchase everything they needed.

When Francis Cabot Lowell built his textile mills in Massachusetts, he hired young, unmarried girls to work. He wanted intelligent, reliable workers, and plenty of smart young women were looking for new opportunities. Some lived on farms, and farm life could be very harsh. The chance to live in a city and earn a paycheck—as much as $3.50 per week—

seemed very appealing. (The average pay for most young girls who worked away from home as "hired help" was only 75 cents per week.) The girls who went to work in Francis Cabot Lowell's factories were called *Lowell girls.*

The Slaters and Francis Cabot Lowell became very rich as a result of their new ideas for making products. They affected the American way of working for many generations. A few people like the Slaters and Francis Cabot Lowell have been remembered as people who started the Industrial Revolution in America. Most of the people who worked in their factories have not been remembered for anything. But without the hardworking Lowell girls and the families who moved to work in the Slaters' mill, the Industrial Revolution may not have happened in America.

The J. P. Morgan family and Nora Nelson lived about 100 years after the Slaters and the Lowells. But Louisa Morgan and Nora Nelson lived the lives they did because of the ideas started and implemented by the Slaters, Lowells, and the workers in the early textile mills.

Changes in Transportation

FOR AS long as anyone could remember, people and products traveled on wagons pulled by animals or on ships pushed by wind. Sometimes people rode on horseback or walked

Workers building the Boonsborough Turnpike Road between Hagerstown and Boonsboro, Maryland.
Courtesy of the Federal Highway Administration, US Department of Transportation

where they needed to go. They used canoes or rafts powered by people. But during the Industrial Revolution, machines began to affect the way people and products traveled.

Before machines became a big part of transportation, overland trails and roads zigzagged between towns and from farms to towns. In some places roads called *turnpikes* required payment at designated stops. When the payment was made, a pike was removed from the road, allowing the traveler to continue.

In 1811 construction began on a road called the National Road—because the national government contributed to the cost of building it. Land was cleared, and men and mules worked to lay down the surface of stone and sand. It took years to build. By 1838 the National Road stretched from Cumberland, Maryland, to Vandalia, Illinois.

The National Road and other gravel roads of the time were better than no roads. But transporting goods and people over roads was slow.

In the winter it could take about seven hours to go 10 miles. The trip from New York to Pittsburgh (400 miles) took a week and a half. Travel from New York to Washington, DC (250 miles) took four days, and travel from New York to New Orleans, Louisiana (1,300 miles) took four weeks. And it could be a very bumpy ride—on a horse-drawn wagon over gravel.

People enjoyed a much smoother journey by river. When Robert Fulton came up with the idea of using a steam engine to power a boat in 1807, river transportation was revolutionized.

Before the use of steam-powered boats, it was fairly easy to travel downstream. The wind and current provided the power. But it was very difficult to move upstream, against the current. It meant a backbreaking and arm-straining job for men who operated river crafts. The only way to move upstream was to use a long pole to push off the river bottom in shallow water and to paddle in deeper areas. The invention of steamboats meant boats could more easily and quickly navigate upstream. This opened up a valuable means of moving products—farm goods and manufactured items—throughout the country. It also meant people could move about much faster.

People were stunned when they heard about Robert Fulton's steamboat traveling 150 miles up the Hudson River in only 32 hours. Steam

Canal boats in Columbus, Ohio.

engines on boats turned the nation's rivers into superhighways. Many rivers wind through the United States. People and goods traveled up and down the rivers constantly.

But sometimes people needed to travel between two rivers to reach their destination. When there were no roads between the rivers, travel was difficult. To solve the problem, engineers designed *canals*—manmade waterways—to connect rivers and lakes or to connect rivers and lakes to seaports.

By 1840 there were thousands of miles of canals spanning the eastern United States. One canal could be hundreds of miles in length. The 400-mile Erie Canal connected the Hudson River in New York City and Lake Erie in Buffalo. The Wabash and Erie Canal—between Toledo, Ohio, and Evansville, Indiana—was more than 450 miles long.

Products such as salt, flour, or textiles were shipped from eastern factories on cargo boats through the canals. Lumber, gravel, or farm products were carried from the West to eastern towns and cities. People traveled on special boats—called *packet* or *canal boats*—where they ate and slept during their journey through the canal. During nice weather they sat on the roof of the boat. This could be a problem, however. When the boat went under a bridge, the passengers had to lie down on the roof to avoid hitting the bridge bottom.

ACTIVITY

Test Machine Travel

BEFORE THE Industrial Revolution introduced new ways of travel, people moved from place to place by foot. The invention of machine travel (steamboats, trains, and cars) greatly reduced travel times. Test for yourself how much time machine travel (a bike) can save.

YOU'LL NEED
- ➤ Measuring tape
- ➤ Duct tape—a bright color will be easier to see
- ➤ A friend
- ➤ Stopwatch or any timepiece with a second hand
- ➤ Pencil and paper
- ➤ Bike

Find a safe place to do this activity, such as a playground, a park, or the school track.

Measure a distance between two points—a distance long enough to pick up speed by bike. Mark the beginning and ending points with duct tape.

Ask your friend to be the stopwatch operator.

First, run between the two points as fast as possible. Have your friend use the stopwatch to record your time. Write it on a piece of paper.

Next, take your bike to the starting line. Ride your bike as fast as you can to the finish line. Have your friend record your time. Write it on the paper.

Compare the two times. How much faster was the bike mode of travel?

"There is a great deal of jolting, a great deal of noise, a great deal of wall, not much window." That's how one person described a trip on a train in 1842. Rail travel was another new form of getting from one place to another in the early 1800s. It may not have been the most

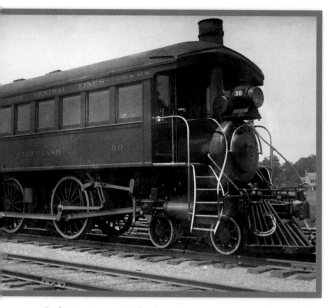

Railroads revolutionized the way people traveled during the Industrial Revolution.

pleasant way to travel, but trains were faster than walking and more comfortable than a horse-drawn stagecoach. And they could travel anywhere that a track could be laid; they didn't depend on a waterway for their movement. At first the rails were made of wood, but later they were replaced with iron rails, which lasted much longer. And coal replaced wood as the fuel that produced steam for the train engines.

When they were first used in the 1820s, trains were considered amazing marvels. Trips that took months by horseback were reduced to days by train. So all that jolting and noise didn't seem so bad. After all, riding in a train car with a roof overhead was warmer and drier than riding in the open air on a horse's back. And train travel did not require ducking under bridges as with a canal boat.

A major transportation milestone occurred when the Transcontinental Railroad was completed in 1869. Two railroad companies teamed up to accomplish the feat, clearing land and laying rails over mountains and rough terrain. Workers for the Central Pacific started on the West Coast and toiled their way east. Workers for the Union Pacific started in Nebraska and worked their way west. The two teams met in Utah.

It's almost impossible to imagine the excitement people must have felt when they began to travel by train. A horse covered about 10 miles per hour in good weather. A train moved at a speed of about 20 miles per hour.

Steamboats, canals, and trains revolutionized travel. But these innovations were just the beginning of the Industrial Revolution. Over the years many more amazing improvements to transportation would occur. New forms of energy fueled new and faster machines. Electricity replaced steam, and gasoline replaced electricity. By the end of the Industrial Revolution, people were using electric streetcars and gasoline-powered automobiles for travel. And those were truly revolutionary.

Changes in the Way People Communicated

FOR GENERATIONS people were very limited in the ways they could communicate. They talked to one another face to face or exchanged letters with people from a distance. Newspapers were a way to distribute information widely and quickly. Magazines and books also spread ideas and opinions. During the Industrial Revolution, people were introduced to new, exciting ways to communicate.

Dear Grand Pa and Grand Ma,

. . . I must tell you how I spent Christmas Eve. We all went to a Christmas tree. I got

SAD HEARTS

The hundred years between 1800 and 1900 were very disruptive for many Native American people and European settlers as two very different cultures clashed. As non-Native people spread across North America in search of new opportunities, Native people were forced to leave their homelands and move to unfamiliar places. Many died. Families were split.

As the Industrial Revolution began, more and more non-Native people tried new ventures. They wanted land and natural resources that were plentiful across the continent. In the South, people needed land to grow cotton to sell to textile mills. In the area that later was known as the midwestern United States, people hoped to grow crops to sell to grain mills. As factories sprang up, large amounts of wood and coal were needed to fuel the vast engines that powered machines. As people began to prefer trains for transportation, rail companies needed land to build tracks.

Many different Native people lived on these lands. As European settlers began to move in, the Native peoples resisted—sometimes taking out their frustrations on the newcomers. By the early and mid-1800s the US gov-

ernment was removing the Native groups from their homes so non-Native people could live without fear. In Georgia, Alabama, and Mississippi the Cherokee, Choctaw, Chickasaw, and Creek left their homes to relocate in western territories. The Seminole left Florida. In the area that would become Illinois and Wisconsin, the Sauk and Fox people moved from their homelands.

The government relocated the Native people to western lands, because most people didn't think the United States would ever expand deeply into the North American continent. But before long, non-Native people began settling farther and farther toward the west. Many of the Native Americans were forced into living arrangements that were foreign to them. Many ended up on reservations.

A Native American leader of the Nez Perce named Hin-mah-too-yah-lat-kekt (Chief Joseph) told how he felt about leaving his home: "My heart is sick and sad." Many Native people felt the same.

Chief Joseph.

a new red oil calico dress and a doll. Uncle Giles put a book on for Sabra and me, and each one of us girls got a string with candy and raisins on it. Christmas Day we all went to Uncle Giles's. New Year's we were invited to a New Year's dinner up to Mr. Bumgardner's. I ate till I nearly bursted—eating oysters and good things. I will tell you what I study: reading and arithmetic and spelling and geography and writing. Christmas night I got a pair of stockings and a nice new book called

The Three White Kittens. Sabra and Maggie both got a new pair of stockings and primer books. New Year's all of us girls got a candy apple apiece and a paper sack of mixed candy and a paper sack of raisins.

From your Grandchild,

Ella "E" Oblinger

Ella Oblinger was 10 years old when she wrote this letter (edited here for clarity) to her grandparents, who lived in Indiana. Ella and her family lived on a Nebraska farm. Although Ella lived during the Industrial Revolution when new, faster forms of communication were emerging, in 1880 most people relied on the US Postal Service to help them keep in touch with family and friends.

Long before the United States existed as a country—in 1692—European colonists settling in North America established a postal service. When the United States was formed, a post office department was part of the new government. It could take at least 10 days for a letter to travel 600 miles. The cost to send a letter depended on the number of pages and

Ella Oblinger wrote a letter to her grandparents in 1880. It took about 10 days for the mail to travel from Nebraska to Indiana.

Courtesy of the Nebraska State Historical Society, RG1346AM

OWNEY, THE RAILWAY MAIL DOG

He was a shaggy dog with gray, yellow, and black fur. No one would call Owney a handsome dog. But everyone who came in contact with this loveable pooch called him loyal and hardworking. He was one of the most famous dogs of the Industrial Revolution.

Owney was a stray that first walked into the Albany, New York, post office in the mid-1880s. At some point the clerks put a leather collar around his neck that read OWNEY, ALBANY POST OFFICE. Before long, Owney began to ride the mail wagon to the train yard where the mail was loaded onto a rail car. One day he hopped onto a car, plopped on top of a bag of mail, and began his long career as the railway mail dog.

Owney rode the rails from coast to coast, hopping off to follow the postal clerk who met the train at each stop. When the mail pouches were safely delivered to the post office, Owney got a ride back to the train where he boarded for the next leg of the trip. If he missed the train's departure, he waited for the next train. But it was reported that he would ride only on the mail cars—no sleepers or passenger cars for a hardworking dog like Owney.

Postal employees all along the routes from New York to Chicago to Cheyenne and San Francisco knew him. People began to attach medals, tags, and ribbons with inscriptions to Owney's collar—so many that he was given a special harness to display them all. They were a testament to the places Owney visited: Nashville, San Antonio, Atlanta, St. Louis, Cincinnati, Sioux City, Portland. He even made a stop at the Minneapolis Industrial Exposition in 1887.

In 2011 Owney was honored by the US Postal Service with a stamp.

Owney, the railway mail dog.

Crack a Code

SAMUEL MORSE designed a new way of communicating. The Morse Code is a system of dots and dashes—short and long sounds—sent over a distance. Develop your own system of communicating in a secret code.

YOU'LL NEED
➤ Pencil and paper
➤ A friend

First see if you can decipher the message below to get some practice and ideas for your own code.

Assign your own symbols to each letter of the alphabet. Share your alphabet with a friend. Then write a note using your unique alphabet. Ask your friend to send you a return note. Translate the note.

Bailey is cool!

---

the distance it was going. It would have cost about two cents to mail Ella's letter to her grandparents.

In the early 1800s steamboats carried much of the nation's mail. By the mid-1800s trains were moving letters and packages across the country. There were special rail cars built just for mail. A man sorted letters on the train as it moved to its destination. When Ella sent her letter to her grandparents, she had to take it to the nearest town to be mailed. Rural mail service didn't begin until 1896.

The use of steamboats and trains to move mail greatly affected communication in the 1800s. People were very impressed with the speed in which a letter could be sent by these new forms of transportation. But there were bigger changes to come, and they seemed almost magical.

Samuel B. Morse wanted very much to be a famous artist. But when he couldn't make a name for himself as a painter, he transferred his creativity to other things. He began to think about electricity and its usefulness as a conductor of sound. After study and experimentation, Samuel asked the US Congress for money to string a wire between Washington, DC, and Baltimore, Maryland. He got $30,000 and put up the wire. On May 24, 1844, Samuel sent a message of sounds that spelled out words across the wire. The telegraph had been born. It was a revolutionary day for communicating.

Soon overhead wires connected cities along the eastern United States. Then telegraph wires began to stretch across the entire country. Eventually wires were laid under the Atlantic Ocean—connecting Europe and America by telegraph. This meant that within minutes a message could be sent thousands of miles—a miraculous feat in the minds of people in the 1800s.

But communication by telegraph was just the beginning. The typewriter sped up the writing process. Phonographs allowed people to listen to recorded music. And by the end of the 1800s people were using radios and telephones to communicate instantly.

Two Stages of Change

MOST OF these revolutionary changes in manufacturing, transportation, and communication occurred during the 1800s. They happened over a period of a little over 100 years. Historians divide the time into two stages: the First Industrial Revolution (1800–1850) and the Second Industrial Revolution (1850–1915). The advances that occurred during the first stage were astonishing. They were stepping stones for the changes that came about during the second stage. What made the two stages different from

WHOA THERE!

Young men who were a little on the skinny side, excellent horseback riders, and willing to give up swearing could apply to become Pony Express riders in the winter of 1860. The newly formed company was hiring lightning-fast riders to carry regular mail and telegraph messages between Missouri and California in 10 days—cutting the travel time in half.

Eighty men and 500 ponies were lined up to do the job. With his messages tucked in a saddlebag, each rider rode as fast as he could for 75 to 100 miles. He changed ponies six times along the way. Each rider was supposed to complete his leg of the journey in six hours. A "relief" rider was waiting to take the mail and gallop away on the next section of the trip.

The riders might have time for a quick meal before heading out for the return trip. Sometimes the stations where the mail pouch exchanges were made were clean and welcoming, with tasty meals prepared by better than average cooks. Others were filthy, bug-infested places where station operators served less than tasty meals—including boiled badger.

It could be a dangerous and miserable trip for the riders and ponies. The weather could be nasty and the route filled with hazards. Some riders carried pistols to defend themselves from human or animal attacks. Others relied on the swiftness of their ponies to carry them from harm's way.

The Pony Express operated for only 19 months. When telegraph lines were completed across the country, there was no need for a Pony Express service. Telegrams could be sent within minutes between Missouri and California. The riders found other jobs, and the ponies were put out to pasture for a well-deserved rest.

Pony Express rider passing men raising telegraph lines.

one another was the *pace* of change. During the First Industrial Revolution, the US Patent Office gave out only 62,000 patents for new inventions. During the Second Industrial Revolution, it issued more than 500,000.

The Civil War (1861–65) was a turning point in the industrialization of America. The advances that had been made in manufacturing, transportation, and communication before 1860 laid the foundation for expansion of those industries after the war. Before the war, 30,000 miles of railroad track had been laid. Thousands of miles of telegraph lines had been strung across the nation. In 1860 about 1.5 million American workers in 140,000 factories produced almost $2 billion in goods. So before the Civil War the United States was on its way to becoming an industrial giant. But during and especially after the war, things really took off.

Before the war America had been a nation of farms. Advances in the design and construction of machinery and tools helped farmers produce more products at a faster rate. In 1793 Eli Whitney and Catharine Littlefield Greene, a Georgia cotton producer, developed a cotton gin that pulled cotton fibers away from the seed. By 1819 plows were made with cast iron rather than wood. Later, steel plows were designed to make it easier for farmers to break up the tough turf on the prairies. After 1840, horses and mules replaced slow-moving oxen for pulling farm equipment. And machines called *threshers* were used to separate grain from the stalk and husks of the plants. By the 1850s steam-powered threshers and plows made growing and harvesting crops a little easier for farm families.

Although farming was still very important after the Civil War, manufacturing began to be a much bigger part of American life. Between 1860 and 1870, the number of factories in America increased by 80 percent. And the workers' output greatly increased. For example, in 1864, factory workers produced 5 million pairs of shoes. Only six years later the number had increased to 25 million pairs. Between 1850 and 1870, mill workers increased the number of pounds of wool they turned into cloth from almost 71 million to over 172 million. Hardworking miners pried 14 million tons of coal out of the earth in 1860. By 1884 they were turning out 100 million tons.

The time it took to do certain jobs was greatly reduced, thanks to new machines and creative ways of working. Clothes were made more quickly after Elias Howe produced a sewing machine in 1846. Farm tools made from iron and steel meant fewer mishaps and shorter repair times. Before 1860 it took 61 hours of work to produce one acre of wheat. By 1900 the time had been reduced to 3 hours, 19 minutes. With 193,000 miles of railroad track stretching across the country, farmers could easily transport their wheat to grain mills. By 1900 the United States had become a leading producer of iron and steel. Oil refining was a major industry.

Over the years people saw astonishing things that they had never dreamed possible. Grandparents told their children and grandchildren about how life had changed. People tried to imagine the next wondrous invention. And some of them used their imagination to bring about more incredible changes. Each generation saw new and fantastic innovations.

Sometimes people wondered if the changes were good for everyone. Adults and children had to work in factories that were unsafe, and the work could be very boring. People lived in big, crowded cities in unhealthy conditions. Many of the workers who operated the machines and built the new roads and railroads lost their lives. About 22,000 workers were killed or injured building the Transcontinental Railroad over the four years of construction. Millions of immigrants left their homes to live in a new country where they faced discrimination. The demand for coal to power the steam-driven machines meant people had to work underground in mines. As factories and cities grew, the environment was affected in bad ways. There were no limits on the amount of sludge a factory could dump into the rivers and streams. Some mine owners didn't worry about destroying the scenic beauty of the hills and mountains. Most people didn't realize the environment was fragile. They thought there was an endless supply of trees, water, and soil. Natural resources were used up, not conserved.

On the positive side, some Americans became extremely wealthy during the Industrial Revolution. Many people from all classes had easier lives because they could buy everyday items instead of having to make them. That meant more leisure time. Families traveled to new places, saw different sights, and kept in touch with relatives and friends who lived far away. Most thought those things were good. The Industrial Revolution made it all possible.

Sometimes people wondered whether their lives were better because of these revolutionary changes. There were those who felt the answer was definitely *Yes!* Others felt *No!* just as strongly. Most, however, thought the answer was both *Yes!* and *No!*

2

NEW WAYS OF WORKING

CHARLES F. STONE must have been excited about starting his new job as superintendent at the S. K. Wilson Woolen Mills in Trenton, New Jersey, on a spring morning in 1895. But his excitement quickly turned to terror as 300 angry women chased him down South Broad Street flinging wooden sewing bobbins at the poor man. Some of the women hit their mark—squarely in the back of Mr. Stone's head.

Mr. Stone had been hired by S. K. Wilson to replace William McGregor, who had worked as superintendent for 14 years at the mill. Nobody told the workers that their old superintendent was being replaced. They arrived at work on May 13 to find Mr. Stone. And they said they didn't like his looks.

It wasn't really Mr. Stone's *looks* that had the women ready to throw their bobbins. It was their unhappiness with the owner of the mill. The women believed the mill owner, Mr. Wilson, had replaced the old superintendent because he had sided with the women when they had gone on strike.

So when the workers learned they were getting a new boss, they refused to begin the workday. They told Mr. Stone he needed to leave. He stayed until the first bobbin sailed past his head. As he fled from the building, the women of the S. K. Wilson Woolen Mills picked up their bobbins and spilled out onto South Broad after him.

By the time the police arrived, the women had returned to the mill. But they still weren't happy. They refused to work until Mr. Wilson brought in Mr. McGregor, the old superintendent, so they could talk to him. When Mr. McGregor arrived, he told the women he didn't want to return to work at the S. K. Wilson Woolen Mills. He suggested they give the new boss a chance. Finally, the women agreed to work for Mr. Stone—on a trial basis.

The women at the S. K. Wilson Woolen Mills were like many men and women who lived and worked in America during the Industrial Revolution. They worked long days, for little pay, and in harsh conditions. For some, working in a factory meant adjusting to a new way of working.

Factory Life

FOR THOSE who were accustomed to working on a farm or in a small shop, factory work could be jarring to the senses. The noise from the big machines was deafening. The buildings were frigid in the winter and stifling in the summer. The workers did the same job hour after hour. It was extremely boring. They usually stood or sat in one spot all day long. They worked 10, 12, 14, or even 16 hours every day. The bosses punished workers who arrived late. The workers lost one cent for every minute they were late, and every penny was precious to them. Some had to stand while they ate their lunch. Others had to go to the cellar to eat. Cellars in factories were usually damp, moldy, and smelly. Sometimes workers shared the cellar lunchroom with mice or rats.

As the Industrial Revolution spread into the 1800s, more and more factories opened. They produced a wide variety of items, including hats, artificial flowers, shoes, cigars, matches, baskets, and brooms. The products varied from place to place. But most factories had one thing in common—unpleasant working conditions.

Making Collars and Cuffs

DOING THE family laundry in the 1800s was an exhausting, backbreaking job. Usually it

Listen to Talking Walls

IT'S LIKELY that most of the businesses in your community today were not in operation during the Industrial Revolution (although some may have been!). However, the *buildings* may have been built at that time. What if the walls could talk? What would they tell us about past occupants of the building? In this activity you will do the work of an architectural historian. You'll give the buildings in your community the chance to "talk" to you.

YOU'LL NEED
- Walking shoes
- Camera
- Pencil and paper (or an electronic device to record your notes)

Choose a section of your neighborhood with multiple business buildings. Choose one building to examine. Or you could tackle an entire block with a group of friends. Get an adult's permission first, then contact the building occupants to let them know what you are doing—especially if you are going inside to record features. Ask them if you can take photographs.

Examine the exterior of the structure. Record the following, either by jotting notes on paper or recording them verbally, using your recording device:

- street address
- building materials (brick, aluminum siding, etc.)
- decorative features
- colors
- name of building and date it was built (sometimes both are engraved on the outside; if not, you may have to do some detective work—city or county courthouse records may help)
- name and type of current business
- signs
- special markings or architectural features (columns, trim, etc.)
- number of floors (including attic and/or basement), doors, windows

Examine the interior of the structure. Record the following:

- type of materials on the walls, floors, ceiling
- decorative features
- colors
- special markings or architectural features (columns, trim, etc.)

Interview the current occupants and/or the owner of the building. Use your camera to snap pictures of architectural features that you find interesting or unique. Go to the courthouse or local historical society to find records for additional information that may be available.

Did the walls (and other objects) "talk" to you? Did you learn anything from your examination of the architectural features? Put your findings into a report. Summarize what you've learned about the building—and include photos and diagrams. Describe the process you used to gather the information. Share your findings with the public library or current owner of the building. Your report will contribute to the history of the community. Future generations may use your data to learn about the buildings and businesses in your community.

Make an Assembly Line Sandwich

DURING THE Industrial Revolution workers learned to work in new ways. Workers in factories learned to do one job and to do it the quickest and most efficient way possible.

In 1911 a man named Frederick Winslow Taylor revolutionized the way factory workers did their jobs. He thought up a way to make workers work better and faster, by applying science to work. He conducted experiments to learn exactly how much time it should take to perform a task without unnecessary steps or motions. Frederick used a stopwatch to perform *time and motion studies*.

Managers in factories began to use Frederick's methods. They called it *scientific management*. Workers were expected to do their job using the one process that the managers had decided was the best. Frederick's ideas are still used in workplaces around the world. You can use scientific management to determine the most efficient way to complete a task.

YOU'LL NEED
- 2 friends
- Pencil and paper
- Bread
- Peanut butter
- Jelly
- Knife

- Stopwatch or any timepiece with a second hand

First you need to do a time and motion study. Ask two friends to help. Think of a task you want to do—such as making a peanut butter and jelly sandwich. Have one friend write down *every single* thing you do as you make the sandwich. Ask the other friend to record the amount of time it takes to do each step.

Look at the list of things you did as you made the sandwich. Have a brainstorming session with your friends about the process you used.

1. Are there steps you could leave out?
2. Are you using motions that are unnecessary?
3. Could you reduce the amount of time it takes to make the sandwich if you cut out some steps?
4. If you eliminate steps, will it affect the quality of your sandwich?
5. With your friends, decide how to be more efficient at making a peanut butter and jelly sandwich.
6. Write down steps for making the sandwich *using the new method* you and your friends designed.
7. Make the sandwich as one friend reads the directions to you. The other friend should record the amount of time it takes to do each step using the new method.
8. Were you able to eliminate motions and save time?
9. Did the new method affect the quality of your peanut butter and jelly sandwich?

You and your friends have applied science to the task of making a peanut and jelly sandwich!

was the housewife's responsibility. First, she got a hot fire going in the cookstove—using coal, wood, or corncobs for fuel. Next, she carried water in heavy wooden buckets from the outside pump. She poured the water into big cast-iron pots for heating on the stove. When the water was very hot, she used it to soak the dirty clothes. Next she rubbed each piece of clothing vigorously against a washboard. Then she rinsed the clothes with clean water that she had hauled in from the outside pump. Finally, she hung the clothes on lines to dry. The next day was set aside for ironing. The clothes were very wrinkled, and ironing was a hot, tiring job. It's no surprise that women were looking for ways to ease their laundry duties.

Hannah Lord Montague lived in Troy, New York, around 1825. As a housewife, Hannah was responsible for the family laundry. While she slogged away each Monday morning scrubbing the week's dirt and grime from the family's stinky clothes, she had a lot of time to think. She thought about how sick and tired she was of washing, starching, and ironing the shirts her husband wore when he went to his office job every day. She noticed that the only parts of the shirts that were soiled were the collars and cuffs. So, one day she cut off the collar and cuffs of one of her husband's shirts. She laundered them and then reattached them to the shirt. It saved a

lot of time because she didn't have to wash the whole shirt.

Historians have credited Hannah with inventing what became known as detachable collars and cuffs. People loved the idea. They didn't own many clothes, so they had to make them last as long as possible. Washing only the collars and cuffs on a shirt made it last longer. And it was cheaper to buy a collar than to buy a whole shirt. So just about everyone wanted detachable collars and cuffs in their wardrobes. And Hannah's hometown became a booming center for the industry.

By the late 1800s over 20 factories manufactured detachable collars and cuffs in Troy, and about 12,000 men, women, and children worked in them. One factory could turn out 600 to 700 dozen collars every day. But it was a complex process and involved many steps.

Workers at the factories made two versions—fabric and paper. They used linen imported from Ireland for the fabric ones. It arrived in huge wooden crates. In the cutting room, workers laid out the fabric on long tables.

Shelves above the cutting tables held wooden patterns. Men called *cutters* placed the patterns on top of the folded fabric. They used sharp knives to trace around the patterns. Each collar or cuff had three parts: two pieces of linen and one piece of calico. Linen was used on the outside, and calico was used inside as lining.

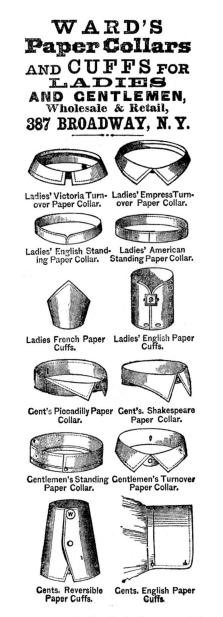

A company named Ward's Collars used Hannah Lord Montague's idea for detachable collars and cuffs to produce products for men and women.

Picture Collection, the New York Public Library, Astor, Lenox and Tilden Foundations

Next, workers took the fabric shapes to the sewing room. There, hundreds of women sat around long tables using steam-powered sewing machines to stitch the pieces together. The tables were only about four feet apart, so the women couldn't move much.

Sometimes the women sang as they worked. One or two women would begin a popular tune. The rest of the sewers joined in with the chorus. The sewing machines were noisy, but the sound of the singing women helped muffle the machine noise.

The collar factories in Troy were typical of many manufacturing businesses during the Industrial Revolution. Men, women, and children worked long hours. They often stood in one place for the entire shift. The noise of

HIDDEN NOTES LEAD TO LOVE

Where did people find true love during the Industrial Revolution? Some factory girls found it through secret messages they hid in the clothes they were making.

Thousands of factories in eastern cities such as New York City, Boston, and Philadelphia produced all types of clothing—shirts, skirts, trousers, gloves, boots, hats, and vests. These items were sent all over the country.

Girls who worked in the factories worked very hard, and their lives could be very dreary. So it was not unusual for a young factory worker to want to change her life. Many thought marriage would make their lives better.

Some of the unmarried girls who worked in the clothing factories in 1895 started having a little fun. They hid notes in the men's clothing they were making and hoped to hear from the men who bought them.

The notes went something like this: "I hope you will be well pleased with this hat. If you have a few minutes' time, please write and tell me how you like your hat. Of course you must be a single man, as I am a single girl. Lovers are scarce in this town."

Men from all over the country responded. Not every girl found true love. But at one factory in Pennsylvania 12 young women found husbands through their hidden note method.

Women sewing in a Massachusetts factory.

clanging machines hurt their ears. There were few breaks from the boredom.

Factory buildings were not designed to be pleasant. The comfort of the workers was not something most factory owners cared about. Very little consideration was given to making the workplace a cheery space. But there were other workplaces that were worse—more cramped, stuffier, and smellier. Those were called *sweatshops*.

Sweatshops

SOME OF the clothes made and sold by factory owners were made entirely in the factory building. But sometimes sewers completed part of the work outside the factory in what became known as sweatshops.

The process started in a factory, where workers did the cutting. Then they bundled the pieces, and people called *jobbers* picked them up. They had contracted with the factory owners to sew the parts together into finished clothes. The jobber hired other people to complete the work. Often they worked in the jobber's home—a *flat*, or apartment, in a building. *Tenement buildings* were huge, many-storied buildings divided into multiple two-room flats. A jobber usually used one room as living quarters for his family. The people the jobber had hired—often women and children—completed the work in the other room. Most rooms were tiny, and some were windowless. One tenement building could house multiple sweatshops.

The tenement buildings were usually located in run-down areas of a city. The people who worked in the sweatshops were desperate for jobs and the money they earned. They worked even when they were sick, because if they didn't work they didn't get paid. Diseases and illnesses easily spread from one person to another. A minister in Brooklyn, New York, described the situation in sweatshops as "as near to hell as anything on earth."

New York City sweatshop, 1908.
Courtesy of the Library of Congress, Prints & Photographs Division, National Child Labor Committee Collection, LC-DIG-nclc-04455

THE RUNNER SCAM

Imagine spending days on a ship with hundreds of people who had nowhere to shower. Sleeping on planks. Having very little privacy when going to the bathroom. Eating stale food. Drinking smelly water. Getting seasick.

Imagine reaching your destination—America, at last! As you take your first step onto the soil of your new home, a man comes to you and says he's an agent of the US government. He insists you follow him to a wagon. He takes you to an unknown destination. When the wagon stops at a house, you are welcomed and offered food. The "agent" demands $2 of your precious savings for the meal. In addition, he requires another $2 for the "immigration tax." You pay because the man is threatening. He takes you to a street corner in the strange city and drops you off to fend for yourself. You are surprised at the way this government official has treated you.

Scenes like this played out often as immigrants arrived in the ports of New York in the years of the Industrial Revolution. Of course, the "agent" was not a government official. He was a *runner* who made a living cheating new immigrants as they arrived. The runner system was one way dishonest people took advantage of new immigrants.

There were caring Americans who tried to disrupt the runner system. The Society for the Protection of Italian Immigrants was one group that looked out for people from Italy who came off the ships. Members of the group wore special hats that the immigrants recognized. They helped the immigrants before the runners got to them.

Lucky immigrants met up with kind, trustworthy people as they embarked on their first adventure in their new home. Those who weren't so fortunate became victims of the runner system.

Arriving at Ellis Island, many immigrants were greeted by "runners" who took advantage of them.

Courtesy of the Library of Congress, Prints & Photographs Division, LC-DIG-ggbain-30546

Many of the people who worked in the sweatshops were newly arrived immigrants. They didn't speak English and were relieved to find work—even in horrible places like sweatshops. But immigrants were easy targets; they were blamed for any problems that existed. They were often victims of cruel and deceitful people who took advantage of them—such as sweatshop jobbers.

In 1899 a government inspector said this about immigrants who worked in sweatshops: "They are filthy and dishonest and have no ambition to improve the situation." He reported that most of the people working in the sweatshops were "foreigners." He blamed them for the problems he saw—"conditions filthy beyond description," "houses full of vermin," and "the worst pestholes on earth."

The official was partly correct. The sweatshops *were* filthy, full of vermin, and pestholes. But the owners of the buildings and the jobbers were to blame—not the poor immigrants who were trying to make a living in any way open to them.

Meatpacking

SLIMY. STIFLING. Filthy. Nauseating. Words not usually associated with food. But many people used those descriptors for meatpacking plants in the late 1800s. They were ghast-ly places to work. And eating meat that was processed in a meatpacking plant in the late 1800s and early 1900s was risky. However, in 1899 it was estimated that every person in America ate about 163 pounds of meat in a year. So meat processing was a big industry. And many men, women, and children worked in the industry.

As the workers entered plants, they often walked over wood floors soaked and slimy with water and animal blood. There were very few windows and little natural light or ventilation. If there were windows, dirt prevented any sunlight from penetrating the cloudy glass. There were no fans, so workers worked in humid rooms heavy with the smells of rotting wood, decaying meat, and stinking animal insides.

Workers brought sides of meat from the cooling rooms to the "boning room," where they were thrown in a heap on the floor. Men stepped over them as they selected one to bring to the worktable for carving. As they cut, they pressed the meat pieces against their bloody aprons and filthy pants.

Scraps dropped to the floor. Workers shoveled them up for ground meat. It wasn't unusual to see men spitting as they worked. The spit fell onto the meat scraps that went into the ground meat. Many of the workers had a serious disease called tuberculosis. The packing

A meatpacking house in Chicago, Illinois.

filler for fresh ground meat. Some plants sold grease made from old, moldy meat to housewives or restaurants.

Managers kept the temperature at 38 degrees in the plant so the meat wouldn't spoil so quickly. But that meant workers were very cold. The restrooms were called *privies.* They were flimsy partitions put up at one end of the workroom—not very far from the meat that customers would buy at the store. Rows of toilet seats—with no walls between them—lined the walls. There was no privacy. There were no sinks, soap, or towels for workers to wash their hands, so they went from the privy back to handling the meat.

In some plants 16-year-old girls stood in boxes of sawdust. The floors were so wet that it was the only way they could keep their feet dry. But there wasn't much they could do to keep their heads dry. The refrigeration rooms were on the floor above them. Water was constantly dripping from the ceiling onto the girls—and into the meat. The girls worked 10-hour days in the damp conditions.

Men and women were sometimes treated differently in the plant. Lunchrooms were rare, so in nice weather men ate outside—standing or sitting on the sidewalk curb. In the winter, they often sat on the meat cutting tables. Women ate in spaces set aside as lunchrooms— sometimes partitions at one end of the work-

plant supervisors said that wasn't a problem. After all, housewives cooked the meat before they served it. They claimed the heat killed the germs before any humans bit into the juicy chunk of meat.

It was common for the plants to store meat in wooden tubs and on carts that were wet and cleaned only occasionally. Meat scraps and grease clung to the sides—accumulating over time—until crusts formed. Dirt and blood stuck to the sides of the containers. The plants stored meat scraps in dark corners on the floor for days. Sometimes they treated them with chemicals and used the scraps as

room. But in some plants the women's lunch space was at one end of the privy.

Meatpacking workers must have asked themselves if the changes in working conditions brought about by the Industrial Revolution had made their lives better.

A Dark and Dangerous World

IT WAS said that some coal companies treated their mine mules better than their human workers. Both mules and men were valuable to the coal companies that provided fuel for factories, mills, and homes during the years of the Industrial Revolution.

Coal was a very important product in America during the 1800s and early 1900s. It fueled the gigantic steam-powered machines in the factories. Mills that produced steel for the manufacture of railroad tracks and farm tools burned coal to run their steam engines and furnaces. Blacksmiths used it to forge tools, and bakers used it to fuel their ovens. Railroad locomotives and steamboats depended on coal to move across the country and through the waterways. Families cooked and heated their homes with it. It seemed everyone depended on coal during the Industrial Revolution. So there were plenty of jobs for men, women, and children in mines where the valuable source of energy clung to the earth.

Coal existed far below the surface of the earth. To get at it, workers had to go underground into mines to pry the coal loose from the mine walls and ceilings, load it into wagons, and haul it to the surface. It was dangerous, dirty, backbreaking work.

The mines provided a variety of jobs. A mule driver cleaned and harnessed the mules early each morning. He hitched the animals to the empty coal cars and took them to the mining areas. When the cars were loaded, the driver returned them to the entrance of the mine. From there the black chunks of mineral were lifted up to the surface. Runners and laborers were important to the mining process too. Runners collected the loaded coal cars and directed the drivers. Laborers assisted the miners. They loaded the cars with the coal that the miner had loosened from the earth.

All the jobs in the mine were important, but the man who held the position of miner was central to the operation. It was the miner's job to actually remove the coal from the earth. His work was the most desirable of all the jobs. Using drills, explosives, scrapers, crowbars, picks, shovels, and hammers, he blasted and picked the coal from the walls and ceilings of the mine rooms. His day began at 6 AM and ended 8 to 10 hours later. Sometimes the miner had to walk a mile from the shaft to the work location. The spaces where the miner worked varied. Some were rooms big enough for two or more to stand and work. Others were narrow tunnels, just big enough to crawl through. Some men worked lying on their side or back.

All the workers in the mine faced constant dangers. There was always the chance of injury or death from cave-ins, fires, explosions, floods, or gas poisoning. The coal dust caused breathing problems. The dampness caused sickness.

Mine workers entered their underground workplace through the shaft, a long vertical channel that stretched from the surface to the area below ground where the mineral lay. An elevator plunged the men through the shaft into the darkness of the cavity. When they reached the bottom—hundreds of feet below ground, they entered an eerie underground world.

The walls were often slimy and moss-covered. A white fungus grew on them. There was a strong smell of smoke, oil, wet earth, and dust. There were loud booms, bangs, and clangs as the coal was blasted, loaded, and transported. Faces and hands were black from the dust, so when workers smiled (and that wasn't often), their teeth seemed to glow in the dark. They all wore hats with lights attached so they could see where they were walking, but it was always very dreary and dim in the mine. No sunlight ever entered their world. It wasn't a job for anyone who feared the dark.

It was a world inhabited by rats too. There were always plenty of the furry creatures in the cracks and crevices of the mine walls and ceilings. The rodents scurried around the men as they ate their lunches. In fact, they tried to get the food from lunch pails. They gnawed the wooden handles of the tools and pestered the mules. Sometimes in the mornings when the workers arrived, they discovered the floors littered with dead rodents that the mules had trampled during the night.

But the men didn't really mind the little pests in their subterranean workplace, be-

Young coal miners inside a shaft in Pennsylvania wearing hats with lights attached.

Courtesy of the Library of Congress, Prints & Photographs Division, LC-DIG-nclc-011448

cause the sight of them meant the air was safe and not poisonous. For some reason that the men didn't understand, rats seemed to know when a cave-in was about to occur. When packs of them began running in one direction, the workers knew they had better follow. Usually the rats were right.

A Better Way of Life?

THE INDUSTRIAL Revolution was a time for change. Men, women, and children moved from their small towns and rural communities to work in new types of industries in big cities. Immigrants migrated thousands of miles hoping for better lives. The changes led to new opportunities. Single men and women could earn money for themselves. Married workers could provide food and clothes for their families. New products were available for people to buy. Families experienced new forms of entertainment. New inventions made life easier. It was a good time to live in America in many ways. But it was also a very difficult time in America for workers.

Some of the bobbin-throwing women at the S. K. Wilson Woolen Mills enjoyed a better way of life than they had in the past. Others were looking for a way out of the factories. The men and women who went to work six days a week in the meatpacking plants looked

BESS, THE MINE MULE

Mules were important to the mining operation. These animals were known for their surefootedness and their strength. They pulled the heavy wagons filled with coal over the damp, uneven floors of the mines. Stables were built in the mines to house the animals. Some mules spent years underground, never seeing daylight. Some mining companies treated the animals well; others worked the animals for weeks or months at a time with no rest—until they died.

The mine workers gave their mules names, such as China, Old Red, Molly, and Bess. Bess was a mule that worked in a mine in Washington State in 1914. She was worked very hard—four months without a break. She worked 24-hour shifts with 10-minute naps. Bess was in poor shape by the end of the four months. Her legs were swollen and bleeding. She had sores on her body. She could barely move as she dragged the heavy coal cars.

Bess was noticed by a newspaper reporter who visited the mine. He reported about her condition. The Humane Society heard about Bess and rescued her from her terrible life in the mine.

A mule inside a Pennsylvania coal mine.
Courtesy of the Library of Congress, Prints & Photographs Division, LC-DIG-nclc-01113

Prepare a Miner's Lunch

MINERS IN the Industrial Revolution had to be creative in preparing their food for underground meals. A popular dish was a meat and vegetable–filled pastry called a *pasty* (pronounced PASS-tee). Pasties are similar to potpies.

Adult supervision required

YOU'LL NEED

Ingredients

CRUST
- 2¼ cups of flour
- Pinch of salt
- ½ cup of lard or shortening
- ¾ cup of cold water

FILLING
- Browned ground beef
- Diced potatoes, carrots, celery, and peas

Utensils
- Large mixing bowl
- Pastry blender or fork
- Rolling pin
- Round pan lid (approximately 6 inches in diameter)
- Knife
- Measuring cups
- Cookie sheet
- Hot pads

TO MAKE THE CRUST

Preheat the oven to 350 degrees Fahrenheit. Mix the flour and the salt in a large mixing bowl. Add the lard or shortening. Using a pastry blender or fork, blend the ingredients. Gradually sprinkle cold water on the mixture, constantly using the pastry blender to make a thick dough. Mix until the dough is sticky and you are able to form it into a ball. On a lightly floured surface, use a rolling pin to roll the dough to a thickness of about ¼ inch.

Place the pan lid on the dough. Cut around the lid using the knife. You should have enough dough to make two circles, which will make two pasties. Set the circles aside as you prepare the filling.

TO MAKE THE FILLING

Combine the ground beef and vegetables. Place about ½ cup of this filling in the center of each pasty circle. Fold the circles in half. Using your thumb and forefinger, pinch the edges of the dough together. Place them on a cookie sheet. Cut small slits in the top of each pasty to allow steam to escape during baking.

Bake in a 350-degree oven for 45 minutes or until the pasties are light brown. Use hot pads to carefully remove the cookie sheet from the oven. Serves two.

forward to the seventh day of the week—a day away from the smell of blood, moldy meat, and rotting animal carcasses. Some of the new immigrants who worked in the sweatshops believed they had arrived in the land that held promise. But they must have had days when they dreamed of their homelands. Some of the men who entered the underground world of the mines were proud to supply the factories and homes of America with fuel. But others hoped for a future that did not include a lifetime without sunlight.

CHINESE WORKERS

The Industrial Revolution in America provided opportunities for Chinese people who were willing to move thousands of miles from their homes. Chinese workers came to the United States to perform backbreaking work building the Transcontinental Railroad in the 1860s. They also worked in fish canneries and mines, and some became servants in homes of wealthy Americans.

Some business owners paid Chinese immigrants lower wages than other workers. This caused problems. Labor unions (see chapter 5, p. 70) complained because their members lost jobs to "cheap labor." They said the Chinese were enemies of American labor because they took jobs that "native" American workers wanted. Some Americans blamed the Chinese workers and took out their anger on them. Many Chinese workers and their families were victims of violence.

Chinese immigrant boys dressed for celebration in New York City in 1911.

Courtesy of the Library of Congress, Prints & Photographs Division, LC-USZ62-37775

The Chinese who came to America for new kinds of jobs faced new forms of discrimination too. Many Americans believed what one union stated in its publication: "We object to them because they never can become good and valuable citizens, because they are impure, corrupt, false, and dishonest."

In 1882 the US Congress passed the Chinese Exclusion Act. Chinese workers could no longer come to America to work. There were some exceptions to the law. Government officials, teachers, students, merchants, and tourists were allowed to enter the country. The law halted the flow of Chinese people into the United States. It was eventually overturned, in 1943, and in 2012 the US Congress passed a resolution expressing regret for passage of the act and the hardships it caused.

3

NEW WAYS OF LIVING

As the Industrial Revolution began to expand throughout the 1800s, people began to live in different ways. Many Americans moved from farms to cities. African Americans left the South for northern and western states. Immigrants left their homelands for America. Cities grew very fast and became very big. Creative people kicked around new ideas. Those ideas became new products that greatly influenced how people lived—in cities as well as in rural areas. It was a revolutionary time in American history.

Slimy Green Liquid Invades City

IN 1892 there was a neighborhood in Jersey City, New Jersey, where the kids were sick all the time. Doctors didn't seem to know what was causing the illness. But parents were sure they knew.

All anyone had to do was walk to the top floor of one of the buildings in the neighborhood and look out the window to the backyard. There they saw a slimy green lake. But this wasn't a resort area. The "lake" was sewer water seeping up into the yard.

The slimy liquid was in basements too. It almost touched the floorboards of the ground floors. Even the street was flooded with sewage mud. At one spot the street had caved in. Piles of rotting garbage lined the streets. Horses, cattle, and pigs dropped dung in the streets. A newspaper reporter wrote this: "It was a scene of filthy, rotten confusion and contagion."

The situation in Jersey City was typical of large cities in the Midwest and Northeast during the Industrial Revolution. There were no sewage treatment systems in place. People tossed their garbage out the windows and doors of their apartments. Cities didn't employ sanitation workers. In some cities roaming pigs ate the garbage in the streets. These unsanitary conditions led to disease. Still, people kept moving to cities from small towns, farms, and other countries. They thought city life in America was better than the places they had left.

The Growth of Cities

CITIES GREW quickly during the Industrial Revolution. Entrepreneurs built businesses in and near cities, because there were thousands of workers available. Different types of transportation moved in and out of cities, so manufacturers could ship their products cheaply and easily.

Families left farms and small towns to live in urban areas. With machines replacing humans on farms, there were more farm laborers looking for work. They wanted new opportunities. Rural life could be very lonely, so cities with their masses of people seemed attractive to many small-town dwellers. Bright lights, skyscrapers, and department stores drew people from rural areas. Cities seemed to have more opportunities. And they appeared to be glamorous places to live.

People from other countries wanted to live in America too. Many immigrants moved from their homelands to America's rural areas, but even more settled in the large cities. There were neighborhoods where immigrants from the same country settled. Those areas were given names such as Little Italy,

Chinatown, or Shanty Town, where Irish immigrants lived.

Immigrants worked in meatpacking plants, steel mills, oil refineries, and coal mines. They worked as servants, mechanics, glassmakers, and shipbuilders. Some worked as cabinet makers, bakers, tailors, shoemakers, and piano makers. Some started their own businesses.

Some Americans treated immigrants badly—just because they weren't born in the United States. Although life in America could be very difficult, many Chinese, Italians, Irish, Russians, Germans, and others believed it was better than life in their homelands. In America there were remarkable opportunities, and there was hope for a better life.

As more and more men, women, and children moved to cities during the Industrial Revolution, the cities struggled to accommodate them. The growth of large cities in America created challenges. In some cases, the challenges were met with peculiar solutions.

Living in Tenements

EVERY DAY thousands of people were looking for places to live in cities. Apartment building owners were happy about this. It meant they could make money renting spaces to single men and women as well as families. Every foot of space was precious. Landlords thought of

Tenement houses were dark, cramped, nasty places to live.
Courtesy of the Library of Congress, Prints & Photographs Division, National Child Labor Committee Collection, LC-DIG-nclc-04078

An airshaft of a dumbbell tenement shown from a rooftop. The shape of the building from that vantage point was like a dumbbell weight— a long and narrow rectangle with wider shapes at each end.

ways to fit many people into small spaces. They came up with creative ideas to get as much rent as possible by squeezing large numbers of tenants into tiny apartments. And they charged very high prices for rent. They came up with the idea of tenement houses—to get as much rent as possible from one building.

Many tenement buildings housed sweatshops, and they also served as homes for families. Each floor was divided into apartments with two or three rooms. It wasn't unusual for 12 to 14 people to share a flat. A family might rent out one of their rooms to a boarder to help pay the rent. But that meant less space for the family.

Sanitary conditions in tenements were horrible. Many people shared one bathroom— usually an outhouse in the backyard. Cooking smells from all the flats mingled, causing nasty odors. The walls were thin. Voices from adjoining flats were clearly heard. Crying babies kept neighbors awake at night.

In many big cities neighborhood after neighborhood was lined on both sides of the street with tenement buildings. They were packed with people. They were so close together that the only windows were at the front and back of the buildings. Very little sunlight entered the rooms. If a flat was in the middle of the building, it didn't have any windows.

Landlords who owned the tenement buildings usually were wealthy and wouldn't be

Design a Tenement Space

TENEMENT APARTMENTS were very unpleasant places to live. Some were only 10 feet square, and an entire family lived together in one or two rooms. How did a family manage to live in such a small space? Using a scale drawing, make a floor plan for your tenement apartment.

YOU'LL NEED

➤ Pencil and paper

➤ Poster paper at least 10 inches square

➤ Ruler

➤ Scissors

➤ Tape measure

➤ Calculator

➤ Tape

Your family has one room that measures 10 feet square. You do everything in this room—cook, eat, sleep, play. Your bathroom is down the hall or even outside in an outhouse and shared with other families. You are lucky because your family is small—dad, mom, and you. Make a list of items you want to have in your apartment. (It's the late 1800s, so include only items that were available in that era.)

Cut your poster paper to measure 10 inches by 10 inches. It represents your 10-foot-square apartment. Use this scale: 1 inch = 1 foot.

Look around your house, and choose items for your tenement. Using the scale (1 foot = 1 inch), cut out shapes from paper that represent the items you've chosen. For example, using a tape measure, find the length and width of your bed. If the dimensions are 3 feet by 6 feet, cut a piece of paper 3 inches by 6 inches to represent the bed in your scaled-down model. Label the shapes

and place them on the poster paper. It may take several tries before you figure out what you can include in your apartment. You may need to be creative. For example, you may not be able to fit beds into the space. Figure out how to sleep if you don't have room for beds. Use your imagination—like the families of the 1800s did—to make it work!

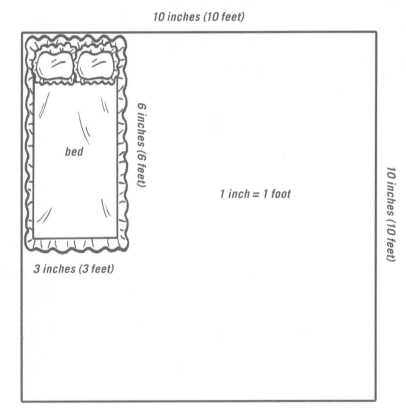

10 inches (10 feet)

6 inches (6 feet)

bed

3 inches (3 feet)

1 inch = 1 foot

10 inches (10 feet)

RATS AS BIG AS DOGS

For 11-year-old Francis Dwyer, March 15, 1893, was one of the most terrifying days of his life. It started when he was walking on the grounds of a hospital in New York City, where he lived. He did something he probably ended up regretting. He started throwing rocks at the windows of one of the buildings. Not surprisingly, the glass in the windows shattered. Francis was caught by a hospital worker and locked in a place known as the "rat room."

"The place was alive with rats!" the terrified boy was reported to have said later when he recalled his ordeal. "At first I didn't mind 'em much, but one of 'em began to nibble at my foot. I was afraid they'd eat me up!"

Francis was released from the rat room after about seven hours. It's probably safe to say he never went near that hospital again.

Rats were a terrible problem during the Industrial Revolution. With thousands of people crowded into large cities and sanitary conditions being what they were, rats lived quite well. They had plenty of garbage to eat. And they were hard to catch. Newspapers were full of rat stories similar to Francis's. There were reports of rats as big as dogs and rats that bit babies in their cribs. Maybe the stories were a bit exaggerated, but for sure rats were a problem.

Rat catcher.

Courtesy of the Library of Congress,
Prints & Photographs Division, LC-DIG-ggbain-00037

caught dead living in one of their own buildings. Some didn't care about the tenants. They didn't make repairs to the buildings. If tenants complained to city officials about the conditions, the landlords issued *dispossess warrants*. In other words, the tenants were forced to leave their homes.

The Age of Electricity

"WE ARE entering upon the age of electricity, and how far it may advance no man can tell…" A writer named Park Benjamin made this surprising prediction in his book, *The Age of Electricity*, in 1886. No one knew at the time just how revolutionary electricity would turn out to be.

There were many amazing advances in science and technology during the Industrial Revolution. But none transformed the world more than the work of Thomas Edison. His experimentation and discoveries related to electricity forever changed the way we live.

Edison was called a genius, and he earned the title by imagining and developing some of the most remarkable objects of his time. His first patent was issued in 1868 when he was a young man of 21. It was the first of many—during his lifetime he patented over 1,300 products. Many of those inventions in one form or another are still used today. The electric lightbulb, phonograph, motion picture camera, batteries, microphone, x-ray machine, and an electric vote recorder were a few of the products that Thomas Edison and his team of inventors designed.

It's difficult to imagine the impact of Edison's experiments with electricity on the lives of everyday people in the late 1800s. In the early 1800s city dwellers rode on streetcars pulled along tracks by horses. When electricity became available, this new source of power replaced animals. New forms of transportation that used electricity—subways underground and elevated trains overhead—were designed. Streets were lit by electric lights. Appliances and machines were powered by electricity. Homes and businesses were electrified. As Edison designed ways to capture and control the power of electricity, the world happily awaited the next amazing invention from this genius.

Edison had so many ideas that he formed a business employing people to experiment and turn his dreams into reality. Other companies hired him to invent products they needed. In some cases, Edison built on the work of other people.

The invention of the telegraph in the 1840s drastically changed the way people communicated. But the invention of the telephone in 1876 was even more astounding. Inventors had been working for years on developing a ma-

chine that allowed people to talk to one another from a distance. But Alexander Graham Bell was the first person to take out a patent for a telephone. Thomas Edison had a hand in the new machine too. He perfected the quality of the sound transmitted through the phone. He also made it possible to use a telephone from a much longer distance than Bell's invention.

A Nation of Steel

NETTIE SHEA and Eliza Trainor were two of 11 elevator passengers who had the scare of a lifetime late in the summer of 1899. The young

Thomas Edison at work.

women were riding in the elevator of a six-story New York City office building early one morning when it stopped on the fifth floor to let a passenger off. As the elevator operator pulled the cable to move to the top floor, the car suddenly began to glide downward. Gradually

A VALUABLE PARTNER

In 1876 as Alexander Graham Bell worked to design one of the most cherished inventions of the Industrial Revolution, he needed the skills of a good mechanical draftsman—someone who could draw the plans that existed in Bell's imagination. He also wanted help getting a patent to protect the work he had completed. In 1884 as Thomas Edison developed his inventions related to electricity, he was searching for someone who could guide him through the patent process—but it had to be an individual who understood the science of electricity. Both Bell and Edison found who they were looking for in an unlikely person.

Lewis Latimer was the son of runaway slaves. As a young boy he learned to read and write. He loved to draw. At the age of 16 Lewis joined the US Navy and fought during the Civil War. After the war he went to work for a law firm in Boston. He worked as a clerk with very little responsibility and low pay. But it was a valuable position for Lewis. Just by watching and reading, he began to learn about mechanical drawing. And because the

Lewis Latimer.

Queens Borough Public Library, Archives, Lewis H. Latimer Papers

law firm helped inventors get patents, Lewis picked up information about navigating the complicated process of applying for patents.

While working at the law firm, Lewis met Alexander Graham Bell. After getting to know the young black man, Bell hired him to draw his plans for the telephone. As he raced to apply for a patent to protect his invention, Bell discovered Lewis was an expert in patent applications. Together, Lewis and Alexander rushed to finish the detailed drawings and complete the paperwork to register the patent in Alexander Bell's name. They succeeded on February 14, 1876.

By 1884 Lewis had been hired by Thomas Edison, who had heard about his expertise in the area of patents. Those skills, along with Lewis's understanding of electricity and electric lighting, made him an invaluable colleague.

Two of the Industrial Revolution's most renowned inventors looked to Lewis Latimer for help and guidance as they ensured their places in history.

it picked up speed as the terrified passengers screamed for help. Miraculously, the runaway elevator car came to a jolting halt at the third floor. The passengers were badly shaken and one of the riders was knocked unconscious, but no one was seriously injured.

Elevators had been used for moving people and freight between floors of buildings since the 1850s. They became more common as skyscrapers began to mark the skylines in large cities. Skyscrapers were made possible because of a new process for manufacturing steel—a stronger, sturdier steel that could safely support the walls and floors of tall buildings. The man behind the new steel was Andrew Carnegie, who became one of the richest men in America.

Steel became a very important product during the Industrial Revolution. Beginning in 1856 it was manufactured using the Bessemer process—named for an Englishman named Henry Bessemer, who found a way to make steel faster and cheaper than in the past.

American Andrew Carnegie saw the Bessemer process used in England and decided to manufacture steel in America in 1873. Not only was Carnegie smart when it came to the science behind steel making, but he also was revolutionary in the ways he managed people and businesses. He was always looking for cheaper and better ways of doing things. He

Model an Elevator

THE IDEA of using pulleys to move objects was not new to the Industrial Revolution. However, elevators and skyscrapers were introduced during the era. This cartoon pokes fun at elevators in tall buildings. The catastrophe illustrated was not likely to happen.

Many machines—including elevators—are operated by a pulley system. The pulleys operate in such a manner that an elevator car would not jettison upward and out of the roof of a building. However, it might plummet to the bottom of a building if a pulley broke.

Elevator cars are lowered and lifted between floors by cables that stretch over a pulley. A counterbalance is at one end of the cable and the elevator car is at the other end. An electric motor is used to operate the system. As the counterbalance moves up, the elevator car moves down. Or, as the counterbalance moves down, the car moves up.

You can duplicate the pulley system used in elevators with a simple experiment.

YOU'LL NEED
- String or ribbon
- Chinese food take-out carton with handle
- Small plastic bag filled with coins
- Spool (thread, ribbon, or fishing line spools work great)
- A friend
- Pencil or wooden skewer

A cartoon showing an elevator crashing through the top of a skyscraper, 1899.

Courtesy of the Library of Congress, Prints & Photographs Division, LC-USZ62-60128

Continued...

Model an Elevator, *continued*

Attach one end of the string to the handle of the take-out carton. The carton represents the elevator car, where people ride. The string is the elevator cable.

Attach the other end of the string to the bag filled with coins. This is the counterweight.

Ask your friend to insert the pencil into the hole of the spool. The pencil should be small enough in diameter to allow the spool to spin. (If you're using a thread spool, you may need to use a wooden skewer rather than a pencil, because the spool must be able to spin.)

With the friend holding each end of the pencil, place the string over the spool. The carton and counterweight should rest on the floor.

Ask your friend to lift the pencil and spool up. As they rise, the carton and bag of coins will rise off the floor.

Pull the bag of coins down and the "car" moves up.

Move the bag up and the car lowers.

By moving the "car" and counterweight up and down, you can see how an elevator works.

owned coal and iron mines, ships, and railroads so he could control the costs involved in making steel. Carnegie's revolutionary ideas made him unpopular with some people—including some workers in his steel mills, where laborers put in very long days for low wages and faced unsafe working conditions.

Carnegie's ideas resulted in steel that was a cheap, reliable—and widely used—material

New ways of processing steel made it stronger. As a result, skyscrapers could be built.

Courtesy of the Library of Congress, Prints & Photographs Division, Detroit Publishing Company Collection, LC-D4-13088

for buildings, bridges, and machines. Much of the steel used in the United States came from Andrew Carnegie's steel mills. That's why he became an exceptionally wealthy man.

The average American citizen benefited from Carnegie's revolutionary ideas. Structures were stronger and safer. Products made from steel lasted longer. Steel mills provided new jobs. Business owners wanted to build new buildings using steel. That created job opportunities for workers in the building trades—painters, stonemasons, architects, engineers, and woodworkers.

J. D. Rockefeller: Cutthroat or Kind?

A MAN named John D. Rockefeller boarded a streetcar in New York City one day in 1897 and found he had no money to pay the fare. A fellow passenger took pity and paid the operator so Rockefeller could continue his journey home. Rockefeller was not to be pitied. In fact, he often stuffed his pockets with dimes and nickels and handed them out to people he met on the street. He was penniless when he boarded the streetcar that day in 1897 because he had emptied his pockets while on a Sunday afternoon stroll.

Rockefeller could afford to hand out money because he was one of the richest men in America in the late 1800s. He had made his money

Andrew Carnegie.

Courtesy of the Library of Congress, Prints & Photographs Division, LC-DIG-hec-16669

during the Industrial Revolution by investing in oil refineries, iron ore and gold mines, natural gas, and other ventures. He started Standard Oil Company in 1870 in Ohio. Rockefeller made a habit of buying out his competitors—sometimes forcing them out of business—so he had very little competition in the marketplace. This allowed him to charge any price he wanted for his products. He also was accused of getting special rates from railroad companies so he could ship his products much cheaper than his competitors could.

John D. Rockefeller giving coins to children.

© Bettmann/Corbis

REPORTER GOES AFTER ROCKEFELLER

When Ida Tarbell was only 14 years old, she felt that a man named John D. Rockefeller had shattered her family's livelihood. Ida's father was an oil refiner in Pennsylvania in 1872. But his business and others in the area were destroyed when a company owned by John D. Rockefeller put them out of business. Ida and many others believed the practices used by Rockefeller were unlawful and just plain wrong.

Years later when Ida was an investigative reporter for *McClure's Magazine*, she wrote a series of articles about Rockefeller and his business methods. Her pieces were read by many people, and they made readers look at Rockefeller in a very negative way.

Ida's articles—published between 1902 and 1904—described how Rockefeller made secret pacts with railroad companies. The railroads agreed to raise the prices they charged to ship oil for everybody. But Rockefeller's Standard Oil Company would get "rebates" from the companies for agreeing to use their rail services. Plus, Rockefeller would get a portion of the rates that the smaller oil companies (like Ida Tarbell's father's company) paid to the railroad companies.

Ida Tarbell.

Courtesy of the Library of Congress, Prints & Photographs Division, LC-USZ62-53912

This was an unfair way of doing business in the minds of some people. But Rockefeller said there was no wrongdoing. He said the railroad companies gave special rates to *all* oil companies—it was up to the company managers to bargain with the railroad owners to get the best possible price. And, he said, Standard Oil Company shipped great quantities of oil, so it was only fair that it should get special rates.

Partly because of Ida's articles, the US Supreme Court ruled on the business practices of Rockefeller and Standard Oil Company. It decided in 1911 that Rockefeller was wrong. It ruled that Standard Oil Company had to be broken up into smaller companies and stop its unfair methods of doing business.

Some of the business practices used by Rockefeller were questioned by other business owners and even the government. He was charged with creating a *monopoly*—having complete control over an industry—and that was not legal. Rockefeller was ordered by the US Supreme Court to break up Standard Oil Company into several separate companies in 1911. The smaller companies would not be as powerful as Standard Oil Company. The Supreme Court decision made it possible for other businesses to compete with Rockefeller. That's how the American business world was supposed to operate—competition was good.

Was John D. Rockefeller a heartless cutthroat? Or a kindly gentleman? It depended on who answered the question—a competitor he forced out of business or one of the many average citizens who benefitted from his generosity over the years. While Rockefeller could be ruthless in his business dealings, he also contributed huge amounts of his wealth to charity—especially in the areas of medical research and education.

A Revolution in Photography

IN THE summer of 1899 well-to-do families vacationing in exclusive Newport, Rhode Island, were fuming about unflattering photographs that were running in newspapers. Men threatened to bring assault charges against the photographers, and women were outraged about photos of them in swimming outfits—without "form improving" corsets. These people were accustomed to seeing themselves in the papers. In fact, they wanted the public to have a peek at their enviable lifestyles. But in the past the photos had been provided by the families themselves—so, of course, only very becoming photos were published. With new inventions in the art of photography during the Industrial Revolution, things changed.

In 1888 George Eastman invented a camera called the Kodak. It was small and used lightweight film to record images. This was a new way of taking photos. In the past photographers had captured images on heavy glass plates, which had to be developed shortly after the photos were taken. Eastman's Kodak allowed the photographer to send the camera to a studio where the film was developed.

Everyone wanted a Kodak. Millions were sold. The Kodak revolutionized photography. Putting cameras in the hands of ordinary citizens changed the art and profession of photography. Everyone could be a photographer. People took up photography as a hobby. They formed clubs, and they exhibited their work in public places. Professional photographers used Kodaks too. It meant they could take photos much more easily. They were able to

snap shots of events and people more quickly. Newspaper photographers captured newsworthy images as they happened.

The rich and famous—who wanted to control how newspaper readers saw them—complained that their privacy was being invaded. Some professional photographers sneered at the amateurs. But nothing could stop the spread of the new invention. The Kodak was here to stay.

As time passed, the role of the Kodak became more apparent. Before the advent of the affordable camera, only wealthy people captured their images and ways of life—through

Not everyone was shy about being photographed when Kodak cameras were new inventions. These swimmers hammed it up for the camera.

professional photographers or commissioned artists. With the development of the Kodak, ordinary people recorded their lives and experiences, leaving a valuable record for future historians. And activists could raise awareness of social injustice by sharing photographs of dangerous conditions or suffering people.

Cars Replace Horses

IN AUGUST 1899 the workers at Montell's Pharmacy in Greenwich, Connecticut, came face to face with disaster. A runaway horse pulling a carriage climbed the stone steps of the storefront and crashed into the door. Luckily, the coachman regained control before the horse made its way into the store, where the frightened clerks hid behind the counters.

Horses in Connecticut and other places weren't used to the noisy, newfangled automobiles that were beginning to appear on streets all over the country. The horse that smashed into Montell's Pharmacy had been spooked by an electric car driven by Miss Helen Benedict, who had been seen driving at speeds up to 12 miles per hour.

In the 1890s more and more automobiles were sharing the roadways with horses. They were considered a novelty and a luxury only the wealthy could afford. It wasn't until early in the 1900s that Henry Ford began to mass produce automobiles, making it possible for more people to buy them.

Ford's automobiles were different than earlier cars because they were built in factories using a method called *mass production*. Large numbers of cars could be made in shorter periods of time as a result of assembly lines. This new way of making things meant that the worker stood in one place while car parts inched past him on a moving surface. The worker completed the same task hour after hour—attaching the front right tire or polishing the rear left fender. It allowed the car to be built much more quickly than before.

An early Ford car.

Courtesy of the Library of Congress, Prints & Photographs Division, LC-USZ62-21222

Because Henry Ford's cars were produced more efficiently, they became very affordable. By the 1920s millions of Americans owned automobiles. Fewer and fewer horses shared the streets with more and more cars.

Life Becomes a Little Easier

EDISON, BELL, Carnegie, Rockefeller, Eastman, and Ford became incredibly rich because they developed products that improved people's lives. Ordinary people strolled city streets brightened by electric lights, spoke to friends across town by telephone, worked in buildings constructed of steel, heated homes with refined oil products, captured family fun with Kodaks, and purchased mass produced automobiles.

The Industrial Revolution was a time when imaginative thinking and daring business ventures combined, resulting in a period of fierce inventiveness. New products were invented, and old ones were improved upon. Business at the US Patent Office, where inventors registered their ideas with the government, was booming. Many of these new gadgets and machines made life easier for people. Some were designed to inject a little fun into dreary lives.

There was the noodle making machine, expandable belt, cotton candy machine, and a new and improved Christmas tree stand.

A woman named Marie Doelle designed a bathtub that could be taken apart for storage. Sarah Breedlove Walker (Madame C. J. Walker) invented hair and cosmetic products specially designed for black women. Annabella Knox made improvements to the design of fire escapes. A black man named Granville T. Woods developed a special telegraph that allowed railroad engineers to communicate between moving trains. Elijah McCoy, the son of runaway slaves, invented a contraption that oiled machines while they were in motion. William Upjohn made medicine taking more bearable when he designed a dissolvable pill. In 1881 Samuel Allen designed a newer, faster snow sled. In 1886 Josephine Garis Cochran invented a dishwashing machine. In 1871 Mattie Knight invented a product that was to become a necessity in almost every store—and is still used today. She designed a machine that made flat-bottomed shopping bags.

With so many new products being invented, it wasn't long before people wanted to get their hands on them. With people eating better, expandable belts were in demand. The idea of a folding bathtub looked good to tenement dwellers who shared bathrooms with multiple families. Who wouldn't want a more digestible pill? And every kid on the block wanted a faster snow sled. It wasn't long before someone came

Josephine Garis Cochran invented a dishwashing machine.

ACTIVITY

Track Manufactured Items

DURING THE Industrial Revolution many different kinds of products were manufactured in factories in the United States. Today many of the things we use every day are made in other countries. Look around your own home to see if this is true.

YOU'LL NEED
- Pencil and paper
- World map (downloaded from the Internet and printed)
- Corrugated cardboard
- Pins with colored heads

Find products in your home that were made in a factory, such as electronics, appliances, clothing, and other items. Find the words that tell where each item was made.

Make a list of all the items and group them by type. Assign a color to each group—red for electronics, blue for clothing, and so on.

Attach the world map to a piece of corrugated cardboard.

Place pins in the appropriate countries to represent the manufactured items made there. Coordinate them by color.

Are there multiple dots of the same color clustered in certain countries? What can you learn about the sources of manufactured goods in the world today? How does it compare to the world of the 1800s?

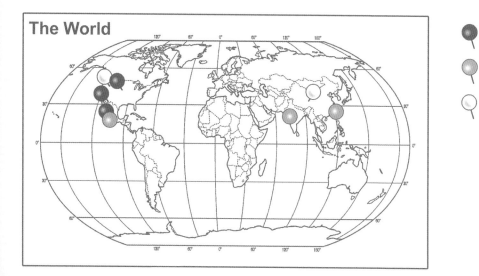

up with a clever way to tempt buyers with these flashy devices and factory-made gadgets.

A New Way of Shopping

As PEOPLE began to ask for the new and improved products of the Industrial Revolution, a new way of providing them also emerged. In the late 1800s department stores became popular places to shop. Stores like Macy's, Bloomingdale's, and Marshall Field's stretched over blocks of downtown real estate and soared multiple stories into the sky. These splendid structures with their grand storefronts and glistening window displays offered a shopping experience unlike anything before. It seemed anything and everything could be purchased under one roof. Hundreds of smiling salespeople were eager to help awestruck shoppers choose from an amazing assortment of finery. Some of the big department stores hired employees who spoke multiple languages to serve the new immigrants arriving every day.

The department store was very different from the general store in the rural areas and the neighborhood shops in the cities. Country stores were small, plain, and limited in the variety of available goods. The urban neighborhood stores generally offered one type of item—meat, bakery items, books, or dry goods. They were owned and operated by one or two people, often the owner and one other person.

The smaller store owners feared the arrival of the showy department stores. They knew they couldn't offer the same products and services as the new enterprises. Many small stores went out of business as shoppers discovered revolutionary ways of getting the necessities—and frills—associated with a new way of living.

No Turning Back

AS THE Industrial Revolution unfolded throughout the 1800s, people began to live very differently than their parents and grandparents did. Many moved from rural to urban areas. They experienced previously unimaginable opportunities. They bought new and unusual products. As electricity and telephones became common, as steel and oil emerged as widely used resources, and as people began to expect products that made their lives easier—the extraordinary became ordinary. The Industrial Revolution changed the way people lived and set the stage for the way people looked to the future.

Inflate a Dollar

IN 1890 a dollar could buy much more than a dollar buys today. Inflation has made money worth less over the years. A dollar in 1890 was equal to about $25 today. In 1890 a dollar bought 10 meals in a restaurant, a full-size bed quilt, or four pair of men's socks.

Use the formula to calculate the prices in the chart. (Of course, many factors influence how much things cost, and "today's prices" below may not match the prices for goods and services were you live or normally shop.)

$1 in 1890 = $25 today

	1890	TODAY
1. Boy's suit	$2.50	$62.50
2. Men's coat	$10.00	
3. Men's pants	$3.00	
4. A 22-inch-by-28-inch decorative framed picture	$3.48	
5. Set of false teeth	$8.00	
6. Cement (Yes, *cement*! Another option was gold—for $1) tooth filling	$0.50	
7. Four-room house	$18.75 per month	

1. $62.50 2. $250 3. $75 4. $87 5. $200 6. $12.50 (cement) or $25 (gold) 7. $468.75

49

The Breakers, the Vanderbilts' "cottage."

KIDS AT WORK

LATE IN JULY 1898, 11-year-old Gladys Vanderbilt arrived in Wickford, Rhode Island, with her parents in their plush private rail car. The Vanderbilt family had just returned to the United States after a long stay in Europe. From Wickford they went by boat to Newport, Rhode Island, where the servants had prepared their cottage, the Breakers, for the family's return. The five-story, 70-room "cottage" was filled with lush plants and fresh flowers from the greenhouse located on the 13-acre estate. Gladys and her family would spend the summer at the oceanside mansion taking advantage of the cool Atlantic breezes just outside their terrace doors.

The Breakers was one of several mansions owned by Cornelius and Alice Vanderbilt. Cornelius had made a fortune as a steamship and railroad builder. The Vanderbilts were a family who had benefited nicely from the Industrial Revolution.

A Different Kind of Childhood

GLADYS VANDERBILT's childhood was very different from that of most children in America in the 1800s. There were few limits on child labor at the time. In fact, in some places the rule was "the younger, the better." Because they were smaller than adults, children were desired in factories—they moved easily between huge machines. And they were paid less than adults.

Children worked in all kinds of factories, making clothes, hats, shoes, ink, and artificial flowers. Children as young as 10 packed tobacco and rolled cigars. They worked in blacksmith shops and fish canneries. They were put to work twisting twine for rope and cutting feathers from birds' tails for ladies' fashions. Children worked in match factories facing constant danger from fires and explosions.

Boys and girls sold radishes from morning until 11 at night in Cincinnati, Ohio.

Courtesy of the Library of Congress, Prints & Photographs Division, National Child Labor Committee Collection, LC-DIG-nclc-03199

Young boys worked in glass factories where they operated fiery furnaces for 12-hour shifts. Children as young as 11 years old bottled beer. The US Census Bureau reported in 1870 that about 750,000 children under 15 years of age were employed in the United States.

The wages earned by children were badly needed in some families. A child sewing knee pants earned 75 cents for every dozen pair he made. A child making cloth coats brought home as much as $1.50 per dozen. A girl working in a dry goods establishment contributed $1.50 per week to the family budget—if she worked at least 60 hours.

Danger in the Workplace

WITH CHILDREN operating big, powerful machines in factories and on farms, serious injuries were a constant threat. But some families were so desperate for the wages their kids brought home they ignored the dangers of the workplace.

Twelve-year-old Charles Neudinger worked in a cotton factory in Pennsylvania in 1885. One day his assistant accidentally started the huge machine that Charles was adjusting. His little body was pierced in multiple places by needles driven into his skin by the machine. Charles had been the main support of his parents, so his death was especially difficult for the family.

ACTIVITY

Take a Break

MANY KIDS spent a great deal of time working so they could contribute to the family's income. But they sometimes found time for play. In the early 1900s Jessie H. Bancroft wrote a book titled *Games for the Playground, Home, School and Gymnasium*. It featured 400 games for children to play at summer camps, gymnasiums, and settlement houses (see p. 97).

Jessie was an expert in physical training, which was unusual for a woman at the time. She founded the American Posture League. Her research was used to apply new principles to the manufacture of school, factory, and office furniture and to seating in subway trains.

Try a couple of the games included in Jessie's book.

ARM'S LENGTH TAG: Two players stand each with an arm extended at full length at shoulder level and try to touch each other without being touched in return. This will require some rapid twisting, dodging, and bending. A touch on the extended hand does not count.

RACE ON ALL FOURS: The performers stand with hands and feet on the floor, the knees stiff, hands clenched and resting on the knuckles. The elbows should be stiff. In this position a race is run, or rather "hitched," over a course that will not easily be too short for the performers.

Long-haired girls working around automated machinery could be a dangerous combination. In 1885 Julia Begley worked in a factory in South Carolina. One day she was cleaning lint from under her machine when her hair got caught in a moving part. Mary Mahoney, working in a laundry in Chicago in 1886, was lifted from the floor when her hair was caught up

TOW BOYS

Streetcars were one of the new forms of transportation that emerged during the Industrial Revolution. And they provided job opportunities for young boys.

Streetcars needed extra help getting up steep hills, and tow boys and horses provided the necessary power. A tow boy had to be agile, quick, and strong. Balanced atop a sometimes frisky horse and carrying a heavy iron hook in one hand and the horse reins in the other, he dropped a big tow hook into the iron loop on a moving streetcar. If the horse was patient, it was easier to get the job done. If the horse was antsy, it could be hard to get the hook in place swiftly.

When the hook was attached to the car, the tow boy yelled, "Giddy up!" and the horse started the long, arduous trek up the hill with the streetcar creeping along behind him. At the top of the hill the tow boy unhooked the horse from the streetcar. It continued on its journey. The tow boy hopped on the back of the horse—without a saddle—and rode to the bottom of the hill to wait for the next streetcar. If the boss was nowhere in sight, the boy might race his horse to the starting point. But that was against the company rules, so usually the trip was at a slower pace.

Tow boys were generally between the ages of 14 and 20. The job was considered a good one, so eager job seekers waited around the streetcars hoping a lazy tow boy wouldn't show up for his 12-to-13-hour shift. There were always fellows looking to take the job. It could be dangerous. It required working in all kinds of weather. But for $1.25 per day, a young boy was willing to endure a little rain, snow, or summer heat. And the danger didn't scare off many hardscrabble boys of the industrial age.

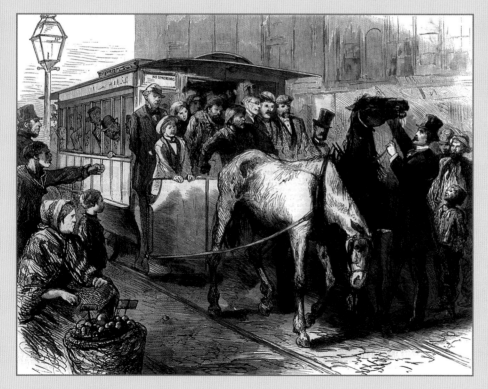

Horses pulling streetcars. An overcrowded streetcar proved to be too much for these horses in New York City in 1872.

Courtesy of the Library of Congress, Prints & Photographs Division, LC-USZ62-63031

in a machine. And Mary Baker was a 16-year-old working in a Connecticut corset factory in 1887 when her hair became tangled in a sewing machine. All of these girls suffered serious injuries. Julia died as a result of her accident.

Factories weren't the only dangerous places for working children. William Frienberg, a delivery boy for a New York City butcher in 1896, tried to jump onto a fast-moving cable car on his way to make a delivery to a customer. The big basket he was carrying caught on a post and William was thrown to the ground. He was pulled under the fender of the cable car. William's injuries were not life threatening—just a broken leg.

Thirteen-year-old Hugh McDavitt was not as lucky. In 1883 he worked for a streetcar company as a tow boy. His job was to handle a horse that pulled loaded streetcars up steep hills. Hugh was knocked down under one of the moving rail cars. His left leg was so badly injured that it had to be amputated.

Breakers, Nippers, and Crackers

"THERE IS no reason why they shouldn't be alive," Barney Dougherty said as he emerged from the main shaft of the St. Paul Coal Mine at Cherry, Illinois. Boy miners Barney Dougherty and Robert McFadden had bravely volunteered to enter the mine where their fellow miners were buried 500 feet underground as a result of a cave-in. The boys had escaped the tragedy but re-entered the mine hoping to hear signs of life farther down where the miners were trapped. The fear was that the men would starve before rescuers could reach them. Fires raged in the mine, and rescue efforts were delayed. Barney and Robert were described by a reporter as "brave lads."

During the Industrial Revolution many young boys worked for mining operations. They started as young as eight years old as *breakers*—working aboveground picking out rocks from the loads of coal that came up from the mines. A breaker worked in a

Breaker boys working in a Pennsylvania coal mine in 1891.

Courtesy of the Library of Congress, Prints & Photographs Division, LC-USZ62-10106

room that was extremely hot in the summer and bitterly cold in the winter. The air was always hazy with coal dust. A breaker's hands became cracked and sore, and his fingernails were worn to the skin from handling the coal, which was as sharp as broken glass. He sat in a stooped position hour after hour—causing some to become deformed and "bentbacked." It wasn't unusual to lose a finger or two in the machinery that moved the coal through the breaker room. That was a known risk of the job. Men with long sticks—*cracker bosses*—prodded or kicked boys who were too slow.

Young boys between 11 and 14 often held jobs as door boys, or *nippers*. It didn't require much skill or strength, so a youngster could easily handle it. Being a door boy was a wearisome, boring job, but it was an important one. Nippers opened and shut the heavy doors as the men and coal cars entered and left different parts of the mine. The doors controlled airflow in the mine, so it was important to have someone opening and shutting them as men passed through. A nipper worked from early morning until late in the day when the last man and car left on each shift. It was not a job for a boy who was scared to be alone in the dark. If he was, he quickly got over his fears. Nippers worked alone all day in nearly complete darkness.

The boy miners found ways to have a little fun during breaks in the grueling work. Some-times they tried to trap the swarms of rats that roamed the mines. And when the cracker boss wasn't looking, they played tricks on him—hiding his hat or prodding stick. Anything to help make the hours go faster in their dark, dank world.

Newsies Spread the News

"Extra! Extra! Read all about it!" It was a common cry heard on every street corner in big cities during the 1800s. The source of all the noise was usually a pint-sized person waving a newspaper high in the air. Passersby heard the headlines for free, but to learn the details, they had to buy a paper. People depended on the newspaper for the latest news, and young boys and girls called *newsies* were on the streets selling to anyone who had a penny or two. Each newsie had his or her own *beat*, or territory. If a competing boy or girl tried to invade another's beat, he or she ran the risk of getting punched.

On slow news days—when there wasn't much news—a newsie made between 60 cents and a dollar for the day. But when there was a big news story like a murder or war, the price for a newspaper jumped. On those days, the newsies could make a whopping $3!

The newsies had to be clever and smart. They estimated how many papers they could sell in a day. After buying daily papers from the publishing company, they sold them on the street for a few cents more each. If they sold all the papers they had bought, they made money. But if they didn't sell every single paper, they lost money. And leftover newspapers were not worth much—except to use as blankets when the sun went down.

Many of the newsies were orphans or abandoned children. They were as young as 10. Many lived on the streets. They slept anywhere they could find a spot to curl up—on the steps of an office building, in a city park, or in an alley. In the winter the best places were on the sidewalk grates where steam rose up and warmed the shivering little bodies throughout the long night. The lucky ones found a sleeping space and a meal at a lodging house.

Not all lodging houses were alike, but in New York City there was one on Fulton Street where boys paid a little if they could. If not, they stayed for free. They got good meals and slept in bunk beds. The first floor was for the boys called "regulars" who had been there the longest. Those were prime spots. Boys who were new—and might have lice—were kept on the upper floors until they were clean. There were lockers around the walls where they put their extra clothing—if they had any. Evening meetings were held for the "improvement" of the boys—they sang hymns or got lessons on

saving money. Sometimes boys who had left came back to talk about their experiences in other parts of the country.

Newsies were often given special treatment. Sometimes the newspaper owner arranged to have them taken to parks for swimming or picnics. Charitable organizations sponsored exclusive outings for them to the beach or amusement parks. Or wealthy individuals contributed to day trips for the newsies—boat

Newsgirls in Delaware, 1910.
Courtesy of the Library of Congress,
Prints & Photographs Division, LC-USZ62-75164

rides or musical events at theaters. At holiday times, they were taken to big halls where they were served spectacular feasts.

Over 500 Connecticut boys and girls were treated by the Burr Brothers, publishers of the *Hartford Times*, to a New Year's party in 1896. The group of newsies gathered at the news offices and was led by a band through the streets of Hartford to Proctor's Opera House. There they were treated to a performance of the popular patriotic play *Old Glory*. The newsies showed their enthusiasm for the play with "noisy demonstrations of approval and patriotism." As they left the theater, each boy and girl was given a bag of fruit and candy.

Life on the Farm

I am doing all the cooking now. Momma is gone up on the prairie, so I do all the work. I washed yesterday and done all the housework. I was awful tired when I first got through with it. But I soon got over that.
—Ella Oblinger

I must tell you about Prince. He just leads right up. I have led him out to water and have fed him. We have gathered 30 rows of corn.
—Nettie Oblinger

I always go with Mama to do the chores. I take a stick and drive old Spot when Mama leads the cows to water. When Papa leads Cole and Queen to water, I go with him. And he lets me ride Cole and Queen.
—Neta Stilgebouer

ELLA, NETTIE, and Neta were children living on a farm in the Midwest in the late 1800s when they wrote these letters to family members

---

A NEWSIE GIVES ADVICE

In 1860 a newspaper reporter from the *New York Times* interviewed a 12-year-old newsie. The reporter described the boy as having "a short nose and a little form." He asked how the boy ended up on the street.

"Well, my dad was a hard 'un. One beautiful day he went on a drinking spree. And he come home and he asked me, 'Where's yer mother?' And I said, 'I don't know.' And he clipt me over the head with an iron pot and knocked me down. And me mother jumped on him—and at it they went. Ah! At it they *went*—and at it they *kept*. And whilst they were fightin', I slipped meself out the back door; and away I went like a scart dog."

Despite the boy's hard life, the reporter wrote that he was "chock full of fun." One evening this newsie was the speaker at the lodging house where he lived. He was seen as a bit of an entertainer by the other boys, who called him "Paddy." But he was serious when he advised the boys to save their hard-earned money. "I hate to see you spendin' your money on penny ice creams. Why don't you save your money? I want you to grow up to be rich men!"

living in other states. The Industrial Revolution had made a difference in the way farmers worked. Steam-powered machines and steel tools made it possible for farmers to work faster and more efficiently. They cultivated bigger fields and produced more crops in less time than in the past. But that didn't mean farmwork was easy. It still required people to plow, plant, and harvest crops; to feed and water animals; to chop wood, haul manure, plant gardens, can vegetables, pick fruit, sew clothes, bake bread, serve meals… The work was almost endless on a farm. And many farms were family operations, where *everyone* helped out.

Children were expected to help with the work on the farm starting at a very young age. Four-year-olds gathered eggs or picked garden produce. Ten-year-olds helped bake bread. And some 12-year-olds were expected to handle teams of horses.

If neighbors needed help, boys and girls were "hired out." Boys worked at neighboring farms chopping wood, hauling water, caring for livestock, or pitching hay. Hired girls cooked, cleaned, cared for children, did laundry, and emptied chamber pots. Wages varied, but in the late 1800s the going rate was around $1.50 per week for hired boys and girls.

When federal child labor laws were passed in 1902 and 1915, they did not cover farm children. So there were few limits on the type of

When child labor laws were passed they did not apply to farm children.
Nebraska State Historical Society, nbhips 16482

work children did on the farm. They operated dangerous machines and tools. They started at very young ages. And there were no limits on the number of hours per day a child could work on a farm.

Orphans at Work

In September 1888 a group of 30 boys from St. John's Orphan Asylum for Boys in Brooklyn, New York, headed west on a train for Fostoria,

Ohio. The owners of a new glass factory in the city had arranged with the orphanage to send the boys. They would have room and board for six months in exchange for working 10-hour days at the factory. After the first six months, the boys would receive wages—$1 per week.

There were plenty of orphans in New York during the years of the Industrial Revolution. Their parents may have gotten sick and died. Or they were so poor they couldn't care for their children. Some were in jail. When children didn't have parents in the 1800s, they might end up in an orphanage—or an "orphan asylum."

The Children's Aid Society, an agency started in 1853 to help homeless children in New York City, began to send orphans on trains to families in other parts of the country. They called the program "placing out." Many went to farms in the Midwest and western United States. Thousands of children were sent to new homes. They ranged in age from babies to teenagers.

The families who took the orphans into their homes agreed to care for them and to send them to school. The children were expected to work on the farm or in the homes. Some families treated the children from the orphan trains like family. Others saw the children as sources of free labor. Not all the orphans who were placed out had good experiences.

When the children arrived at the train station, they were lined up on the platform. They were looked over by the potential new parents. Some checked their teeth. Others felt their arm muscles. When this happened, it made the orphans feel like animals at a livestock auction.

Just before Christmas in 1896, eight boys and two girls arrived in Sumner, Iowa, from New York. They were taken to the Cass Opera House, where local citizens listened to Mr. E. Trott from the Children's Aid Society describe the work of the association. He gave a history of each of the children and explained how all could be adopted. Mr. Trott explained what was required of the adopting parents. The children were to be well clothed, given moral and educational advantages, and stay with the family until they reached 18 years of age. By the end of the event, all the children had been taken. Several citizens went home disappointed because there were not enough orphans for everyone who wanted one.

In Chicago an ad was published in a newspaper announcing the need for homes for 18 children. There were 8 boys and 10 babies available, ranging in age from one month to 10 years. It was possible to get a child for 90 days on a trial basis. They were described as "good looking" and "intelligent" and "very promising."

With thousands of orphans riding the orphan trains over the years, it was expected that there would be mixed results as far as the success of the program. The Children's Aid Society tried to make sure the children found happy homes. They asked the children and their new families to keep in touch with the New York office by mail. Workers from the society visited the children in their new homes periodically. If there was an unhappy situation, they tried to change things. Children might be moved to a different family. Some older children ran away from their unhappy circumstances. They took their chances on their own rather than staying in a bad home.

Little Time for School

WITH CHILDREN working long hours all year long in factories, in mines, and on farms, there was very little time left for school. For some kids, going to school was a luxury. Being able to read, write, or do math wasn't necessary for most jobs. Strength and stamina were more important qualities for the types of jobs available during the Industrial Revolution.

Even some school officials doubted that schooling for children was very practical. In 1890 the New York state superintendent of schools said, "It is worse than futile to assume

that all persons charged with the care of children will send them to school."

Most states required children to attend school. But the children didn't have to go to school for very long. Many people ignored the laws. They were difficult to enforce. It wasn't always clear *who* should enforce the school laws. The schools? Police? Parents?

In Massachusetts, children between 8 and 14 years of age were required to attend school. But they had to go for only 12 weeks per year. In 1894 New York passed a law that

Schoolchildren in Washington, DC, circa 1899.

Courtesy of the Library of Congress, Prints & Photographs Division, LC-USZ62-90603

Create an Early-1900s Diary

BOOKMAKING WAS a very important business in American factories during the Industrial Revolution. Many kids worked in book manufacturing. Try your hand at making your own paper and book—a diary of an Industrial Revolution–era kid.

Adult supervision required

YOU'LL NEED

- Scissors
- Piece of window screen at least 5 inches by 7 inches. Screen can be purchased at hardware or home improvement stores.
- Staple gun or hammer and ½-inch nails (or smaller, depending on the thickness of the picture frame); the nails should not extend beyond the thickness of the frame.
- A 5-inch-by-7-inch wood picture frame with the glass removed
- Old newspapers
- Large bowl of water
- Kitchen blender
- 2 teaspoons of liquid laundry starch
- Cake pan or casserole dish that is larger than the picture frame
- Wooden spoon
- Large bath towel
- Spatula
- Hair dryer
- Iron and ironing board
- Brown paper bag or construction paper— crumpled and then smoothed (to look rustic)—to serve as the cover
- Hole punch
- String or ribbon
- Pencil

TO MAKE THE DIARY

Cut the screen to the same size as the outside of the frame. Attach the screen tightly to the picture frame using the staple gun or a hammer and nails.

Tear newspapers into small pieces and soak them in a large bowl of water for 30 minutes.

Fill the blender half full with the wet newspaper scraps. Add warm water to the blender until it is full. Blend the mixture until it is a fine texture. Finer texture will make the paper smoother and easier to write on.

Add 2 teaspoons of liquid laundry starch to the blender and mix. The mixture will be similar to a bowl of thick cooked oatmeal.

Fill the cake pan or casserole dish half full of water. Add the paper mixture from the blender. Stir with a wooden spoon.

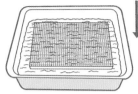

Place the frame in the cake pan. Jiggle the mixture so it evenly covers the screen.

Lift the frame from the pan. Hold it over the pan to drain excess water. (This may take a few minutes.)

Place the frame on a large bath towel. Use a spatula or similar object to press the paper down on the screen to squeeze out more water. Keep the pulp as flat and smooth as possible. The towel will soak up the water as you press down.

When you have removed as much of the water as possible, let the paper dry. This could take several days, depending on the thickness of your pulp. You can speed the drying process by gently blowing the paper with a hair dryer.

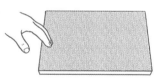

Monitor the drying process. When the sheet can be easily removed from the screen, carefully pull it up. A spatula may be helpful.

If the sheet is still damp, continue drying it on a flat surface. An adult can help iron the paper using an iron on low temperature. This will make the surface of your paper smoother.

After the paper has dried completely, cut it into several pages of equal size.

Use the brown paper bag to make the book's cover. Put the pages and cover together 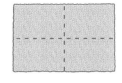 in the form of a book. Punch holes in the far left-hand edge of the book.

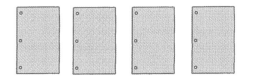

Place string or ribbon through the holes and tie it tightly to bind the book.

Your homemade diary is ready to hold your thoughts.

Brother and sister Uriah and Eva Westbrook in 1914.

TO KEEP A PERIOD DIARY

Meet Uriah and Eva Westbrook, a brother and sister who lived and worked in a cotton mill in North Carolina in 1914. First, decide if you will write as Uriah or Eva, and imagine what their lives must have been like. The photograph can help to activate your imagination. Does the family have plenty of money? Are they happy? How old are they? What kind of house do they live in? How many people are in the family?

Provide readers with your selected child's basic facts such as age, siblings, parents, and best friend. Use your imagination to keep a diary of his or her daily activities for a week. Make the diary look like it may have in 1914. Write in pencil. Create drawings to add interest to the document.

required every child between the ages of 8 and 16 to attend school to learn reading, writing, spelling, arithmetic, grammar, and geography. But even the laws seemed to place more value on work than school. Teenagers between 14 and 16 who had jobs didn't have to go to school. Children between 12 and 14 were given a break: they were required to attend school for only 80 consecutive days all year if they were employed.

In New York, business owners weren't supposed to hire children between the ages of 8 and 12 while school was in session—October to June. And they couldn't hire 12- to 14-year-olds without a certificate saying the child had attended school for the required amount of time.

The schools employed attendance officers to enforce the laws. Parents were fined $5 for the first offense. A second offense resulted in a $50 fine or 30 days in jail. Children who constantly avoided school were put in a special truant school.

Not everyone liked the idea of requiring children to attend school. Some business owners didn't like the school laws. Kids were a source of cheap labor—at least for a few weeks each year. Some parents wanted the money the working children brought into the household more than they wanted an educated child. Other people were concerned that making all those kids attend schools would put a burden on the teachers and the school budgets. Mandatory education was a controversial topic during the Industrial Revolution.

NAUGHTY BOYS

Williston Seminary, an all-boys boarding school in Massachusetts, had a new principal in 1878. As new principals often do, Mr. J. M. Whiton made a few changes. Some were not well received by the students. The most unpopular rule was the one that said students could not associate with the girls who worked at the local factory.

One Saturday the boys decided to let the principal know how unhappy they were about the new policy. After dark a group of students snuck out of their rooms and went to the principal's house. It had a big, wide porch with white columns. Armed with red and blue paint, the mischievous boys painted stripes all around the columns—making them look like barbershop poles. They also put signs across the front of the house advertising prices for shaves and haircuts.

The next day the principal asked the school's teachers to help uncover the column painters. Teachers searched the boys' rooms—rummaging through dresser drawers, trunks, and suitcases. They found clothes spattered with red and blue paint in some rooms. The culprits were exposed!

The students were furious that the teachers had snooped through their belongings. An invasion of their privacy! There were 190 students at Williston, and 130 of them gathered at a mass meeting to protest. They threatened revenge on Mr. Whiton. The principal took them seriously and had four watchmen at his house that night. Fortunately, no additional vandalism was done.

The Hearn family, owners of James A. Hearn & Co.—one of the largest department stores in New York City in the late 1800s—valued education for *their* young workers. The company was known as one of the more progressive businesses in the city. In the early 1900s it was one of the first stores to use motorized vehicles to make home deliveries. With its fleet of 40 "machines," drivers made deliveries throughout the city from 8 AM to 7 PM. The Hearns were very modern and forward thinking in many respects.

The department store was known not only for its delivery service. Like many stores, the company employed children, who worked from morning until closing—as late as 10 PM some days. That left very little time for school.

The Hearn family decided to do something about that. One of the upper floors of the store was converted into a school. There were so many children working at the store that they went to school in shifts. When one group finished their lessons, another made their way to the top floor schoolrooms. They learned reading, writing, arithmetic, spelling, history, and deportment (manners).

Some of the children were eager to attend the store school because they liked to learn. But they had another reason for looking forward to the school lessons. They earned job promotions and raises based on their performance in the department store school!

Giving Kids a Break

AS THE years of the Industrial Revolution evolved, some adults realized that kids should spend their days in schools, not in stuffy factories and dangerous mines. They understood that kids should play in grassy parks, not in streets littered with garbage. They explored different ways to help parentless kids. And by the early 1900s they passed laws to protect kids. Not every child could live like the privileged Gladys Vanderbilt, but fewer would live like Barney Dougherty, the boy miner, or Mary Baker, the girl who lost her hair in a corset factory.

CATASTROPHES, UNIONS, AND STRIKES

MOST PEOPLE WOULD THINK working in a candy factory was a dream job, but it turned out to be a nightmare for the employees of the Diamond Candy Company in Brooklyn, New York, in 1915. On Saturday, November 6, Harry Koop, a shipping clerk at the factory, was working in his office when he looked up to see flames shooting up the walls in the hallway. About the same time, a policeman patrolling in the neighborhood saw flames and heavy smoke pouring from the first- and second-floor windows and called the fire department. By the time firemen arrived, workers were jumping from the upper floors of the five-story building. Witnesses heard the screams and cries for help. A young girl shouted from a fifth-floor window, "Help, oh, help us!"

Harry Koop and most of the other workers escaped the burning building. Thirty-eight workers were injured—many as they jumped from windows to life nets. Some didn't wait for nets and plunged to the brick street. Twelve people died. Nineteen-year-old Bertha Rossman, 17-year-old Rose Goldman, and 10-year-old Cecelia Brook were among the dead.

When survivors told their stories, investigators learned that the fire was fed by hundreds of cardboard boxes stored in a hallway. Even more disturbing was the claim by workers on the upper floors. They said the doors were locked—keeping them from leaving the burning building through the stairways. The building had only one fire escape for over 200 employees.

The *Pittsburgh Press* newspaper reported this was the fifth fire at the building in four years. Safety inspectors had ordered the owners of the building to make repairs, but they had been ignored. The Diamond Candy Company fire occurred in 1915. But unsafe conditions had existed in factories for many years.

A Long History of Tragedy

DAY AFTER day, month after month over the years of the Industrial Revolution, the men, women, and children who toiled in the factories and mines of America risked their lives just by going to work.

Newspaper headlines captured the stories of terror and turmoil:

> FLAMES IN A TOBACCO FACTORY—
> 400 PERSONS THROWN OUT OF
> EMPLOYMENT
> EXPLOSION IN BOSTON FIREWORKS
> FACTORY—SIX MEN AND BOYS
> BURNED TO DEATH

Firemen on their way to a factory fire in New York City in 1911.

Courtesy of the Library of Congress, Prints & Photographs Division, LC-USZ62-34985

LARGE FACTORY BURNED—WOMEN
SPRINGING FROM WINDOWS
APPALLING CALAMITY! MEN HURLED
THIRTY FEET IN AIR

The five children of Thomas Healy lost their father to an explosion in a gunpowder factory at Saugerties, New York, in May 1854. Thomas was one of seven men who lost their lives in the catastrophe. The explosion was heard for miles around as more than 600 kegs of powder were ignited. It wasn't the first incident to occur at the Laflins & Smith establishment, but none before had resulted in such loss of life.

Six years later the *New York Times* newspaper described a disaster scene as "unspeakably hideous" and reported that the dead were "the most fortunate of the victims." The top five stories of Pemberton Mill at Lawrence, Massachusetts, had collapsed onto the 700 workers on the lower floors. Observers could hear the cries of those buried in the rubble. As rescuers labored to remove survivors from the ruins, night began to fall. It was January 1860, and they had built bonfires around the site to help with the rescue efforts. Somehow the fires spread to the piles of wreckage—where many of the survivors were trapped. Mangled limbs prevented them from escaping the jumble of debris. The worst possible scenario unfolded

as the imprisoned workers who had survived the collapse of the building were consumed by the flames. Little could be done to help them. Some blamed the disaster on shoddy construction of the mill building. Workers believed the foundation was imperfect and the walls were weak. The floors were not designed to hold the heavy machinery or the vast number of workers.

Carpenter John Woods was working in a fireworks factory in Boston, Massachusetts, in June 1875 when he sensed that something terrible was about to happen. Being near a window, he jumped to the street below and ran. When he was about 20 feet from the factory, a massive explosion tore through the building, sending debris and human beings into the air. The building was completely engulfed in flames by the time the fire department arrived. Only 10 men and boys were employed at the business. Six of them died. The others were seriously burned. John Woods was the only lucky one.

It was a common practice to use lard—animal fat—in cooking in the 1800s. Karscher & Paul's was a lard processing plant in Brooklyn, New York. In the spring of 1885, while four workers were tending the plant, a large tank of boiling lard exploded. The blast was so powerful that an entire section of the building was demolished. Three of the workers were injured. But a young boy—Johnny Kramer—was killed. His parents sued the owners for $10,000. The *New York Times* reported that only a month before the tragedy a building inspector for the city had condemned the structure. Workers reported that the hot tank was suspended from the third-floor ceiling beams. And they said the floor was soaked with grease and oil.

Fortunately, most of the women who worked at the factory in Plymouth, Pennsylvania, that made squibs—explosives used by miners to loosen coal from mine walls—were at home for their lunch break on February 25, 1889. But 15-year-old Gladys Reese, 16-year-old Jane Ann Thomas, and 17-year-old Maggie Richards had stayed in the factory for lunch and were among the dead at the end of the day. Those workers who were enjoying lunch at home were disturbed by "deafening thunders of a terrific explosion" and ran to their windows where they saw clouds of smoke over the factory. Rushing to the scene, they watched in horror as their fellow workers—covered in blood and gasping for air—appeared at the windows of the burning building. Their frantic cries for help were heard by coal miners at a nearby mining operation who attempted to free the terrified girls. But a second explosion forced the rescuers back as the building collapsed, burying the trapped workers. Eleven girls were killed that day in the tragedy that left the community with a "death-like pall" hanging over the town.

All these horrific tragedies occurred over about 100 years. Were they caused by faulty building practices or by negligence on the part of the factory owners? Could they have been avoided? In most cases, those questions were never answered. But, as the years of the Industrial Revolution unfolded, workers began to ask questions that made people uncomfortable. They talked about conditions in the factories, mills, and mines. And they became angry when they saw unsafe situations that they knew caused catastrophes. It made America's workers want to do something about unnecessary accidents in their workplaces. As the Industrial Revolution moved into the late 1800s, workers decided to take action.

A Long History of Unions

IN THE 1800s as American workers faced 14- to 16-hour days with low pay, they began to ask, How can we spend more time with our families? When they lost their jobs because of illness, they asked, Is this fair? As they saw friends jump from burning factory buildings to their deaths, workers asked, Why does my boss force me to work in dangerous conditions? As they searched for answers, many decided to do something about their situations.

In 1827 a group of carpenters in Philadelphia were sick and tired of working from sunup to sundown six days a week. They were exhausted by Sunday. They had very little time to help out in their communities. They were too busy to play with their children. The carpenters thought they deserved better lives.

In October they invited other workers in the building trades to form a *labor union*—a group of workers who joined together to work for common goals. The Mechanics' Union of Trade Associations included bricklayers, painters, glaziers, and other craftsmen. They published a newspaper called the *Mechanics Free Press*. When union members' families needed food or money, the union helped them. The union tried very hard to force business owners to limit the workday to 10 hours. It took years for them to accomplish this goal. Finally, in 1837 the city of Philadelphia passed a law that limited the workday to 10 hours.

Labor unions were organized in Boston, New York City, Baltimore, and other cities during the 1830s. Sometimes a union included only one craft or profession, such as laundry workers or shoemakers. Others might consist of workers from different professions united in one union, such as carpenters, painters, and bricklayers.

Women who worked in the textile mills of the northeastern part of the United States formed unions called female labor reform associations. The first was started by Sarah Bagley, Huldah Stone, Hannah Tarlton, Mary Emerson, and Sarah Young in Lowell, Massachusetts, in 1845. The Lowell Female Labor Reform Association fought for a 10-hour day, more time for meals, and better ventilation in the mills. Sarah Bagley, a "woman of unusual charm and ability," was the president of the group. Huldah Stone wrote articles for the workers' newspaper called the *Voice of Industry*. Huldah wrote, "Now is the time for action." The women formed a committee to watch for articles in local newspapers that contained false or inaccurate information about mill workers. They tried to address these inaccuracies. They wrote letters, passed out pamphlets, and made speeches that explained their hopes for better working conditions.

Female labor reform associations were started in other cities too. They were modeled after the group in Lowell. Elizabeth Gray, Mary Graham, and Annie S. Stevens gathered tailors, cap makers, shirtmakers, bookbinders, and lace makers to form the Female Industrial Association of New York in March 1845. They said they were taking upon themselves "the task of asserting their rights against unjust employers." In Massachusetts, sixty women and girls formed the Female Labor Reform Association of Manchester in December 1845. In less than a year the membership had grown to 300. Under the leadership of Sarah Rumrill, the women printed pamphlets and held public lectures asking for shorter hours and better pay.

Shipbuilding was a big industry in the 1800s. It provided jobs for many people. Ships were made of wood. An important step in building a ship was sealing the spaces between the wooden planks so they were watertight. Men who did this work were called *caulkers*. The job required a great deal of skill. Many free African Americans worked as caulkers in Baltimore, Maryland, in the early 1800s. In 1838 they formed a union called the Caulkers Association. It helped members get very good wages for the time—about $1.75 per day. Many shipbuilders hired these men because they knew they were skilled.

The caulker profession looked to quite a few people like an attractive way to make a living. When some white people saw how much money the African American caulkers were making, they became jealous and wanted those jobs. In the 1850s shipbuilding companies started hiring white Americans and German and Irish immigrants as caulkers. They weren't always as skilled as the African American members of the Caulkers Association.

In the early 1860s white ship workers in Baltimore tried to force shipyard owners to fire all their black caulkers and hire whites to replace them. The union of white ship workers in the city fined members who worked with black caulkers. In 1865 white workers went on strike, forcing shipbuilders to stop hiring African American caulkers. It became very difficult for the black caulkers to find work.

Isaac Myers, an African American living in Baltimore, had worked as a caulker when he was young. He became a successful businessman. Isaac knew how important caulking was to shipbuilding. He was determined to help unemployed African American caulkers continue to work. In 1868 he started a shipping company that built and repaired ships. He hired hundreds of African American caulkers.

Isaac was very active in African American labor unions. In 1868 he helped start the Colored Caulkers' Trade Union Society of Baltimore. A year later he organized workers from several different trades into the Colored National Labor Union. And in 1875 Isaac helped form the Colored Men's Progressive and Cooperative Union in Baltimore. Women were allowed too. Workers from various trades joined. They fought for equal pay and opportunities for black workers.

In the early 1800s workers formed hundreds of labor unions. Most were local groups, operating in one city or region. Some lasted only a few years. Some failed to accomplish their goals. But all who joined these early unions—across many different professions—believed what the women of the female labor reform associations of New England had written in the 1840s: "Union is strength." These brave men and women helped lay the foundation for larger, national unions that came later—and that would revolutionize many industries.

Revolutionary Unions

MANY OF America's working men and women in different areas of the country believed that labor unions gave them the power. Unions could win better wages, shorter days, and safer conditions for workers. The members of the Mechanics' Union of Trade Associations in Pennsylvania, Lowell Female Labor Reform Association in Massachusetts, and Caulkers Association in Maryland made life better for a few people in regions of the nation. But many Americans understood that for workers—across the country and in all types of industries—to have real power, they needed *national* unions.

Workers from six different cities and a variety of local craft unions came together in

Create a Time Line of Your Life

HISTORIANS USE time lines to help put events in order. It is easier to understand the past if we understand the order of events and if we know what events happened in relation to others. It helps to know who was interacting with whom at the time. Create a time line of events from your life along with people, places, and happenings from around your state, nation, and the world. Do events outside your school/home/community affect you? How? Do you see cause-and-effect situations? In other words, do things that happen cause other things to happen?

YOU'LL NEED
➤ Photographs or artifacts such as printed programs from school events, news clippings from sporting events, or medals you've won that help to tell the story of your life
➤ Ruler or straightedge
➤ Marker
➤ A long sheet of paper, about 3 feet long (from a crafts store or a meat counter at a food store)
➤ Tape or glue stick

Gather artifacts and photos of your life. Using the ruler or straightedge, draw a straight horizontal line across the center of the sheet of paper.

At the far left-hand side of the line, write the year you were born. On the far right-hand side, write the current year.

Tape or glue your artifacts (including dates of the event related to your artifact) along the time line.

Add important world and national events and important people to the time line, and include the dates associated with each. This will help you to understand what was happening in the world beyond your immediate world.

August 1834 in New York City. They formed the first union with a national focus—the National Trades' Union (NTU). It worked to improve conditions for children in textile mills, and it fought to limit the workday to 10 hours.

But the NTU didn't last long. By 1837 it had died out.

In 1866 another attempt was made to start a nationwide labor union. A group gathered in Baltimore, Maryland, to form the National Labor Union (NLU). It included workers from different professions. Both skilled and unskilled workers were welcome. Black workers and women joined, which was unusual for the time. At first it was very successful. Over 600,000 joined the NLU. They tried to get the US Congress to pass a law limiting the workday to eight hours. They fought for equal pay for women.

The NLU was successful in getting an eight-hour day for government workers. But workers in private companies still worked 10 or more hours per day, and women workers continued to earn less than men. In 1869 the NLU members decided they didn't want black members. It forced those workers to form a separate union, called the Colored National Labor Union. Like the NTU, the NLU began to lose members after a few years. By the mid-1870s it had disappeared. But another group secretly began to tempt unhappy workers, and it would fill a gap left by the NLU.

"Shhh, it's a secret." In 1869 a group of garment workers led by Uriah Smith Stephens met in secret in Philadelphia to form the Noble and

KNIGHT FACES DISCRIMINATION

Frank J. Ferrell was a member of the Knights of Labor in New York City in 1886. He was chosen as a representative to the Knights' yearly convention, which was in Richmond, Virginia, that year. When Frank and the other Knights from New York City tried to check into their hotel in Virginia, they were told that Frank would not be welcome. So Frank and some of the other Knights from New York camped out in tents. Later that night Frank and some of the other Knights went to a theater to see a musical performance. When Frank sat down, many of the audience members got up and left.

Why were people in Virginia acting so strangely when Frank appeared? For one reason: Frank was African American. Although slavery had ended many years earlier, some people discriminated against African Americans.

Frank faced more discrimination when he got to the Knights of Labor convention. Some members wanted him to introduce a speaker—the governor of Virginia—to the convention audience. It was a great honor. Others knew that the governor would have been highly insulted to share a stage with an African American and to be introduced by him. The Knights didn't want to make the governor angry, so they came up with a solution. Frank introduced the head of the Knights of Labor union, who in turn introduced the governor.

Although the Knights of Labor welcomed African Americans, they refused to stand up for Frank Ferrell's civil rights.

Holy Order of the Knights of Labor. It would become one of the first successful national labor unions in the United States. At the time, joining a union could mean trouble. Business owners didn't like unions. They didn't want their employees joining them. They didn't want union members demanding higher wages and shorter days. Sometimes business owners fired workers who joined unions. They hired spies to get information about union organizers. So when the Noble and Holy Order of the Knights of Labor started, they chose a secret password. People coming to the meetings had to give the password or they couldn't get in the meeting hall. It was intended to keep spies out.

The organization was open to all—skilled craft workers and unskilled laborers. Blacks, women, and immigrants were encouraged to join. Thousands of blacks joined. But in southern states many black workers who tried to become Knights of Labor members met with violence.

At first the union grew slowly. When the Knights of Labor stopped meeting in secret, membership grew much faster. By 1886 over 700,000 men and women across the country were members. Things began to change a few years later. A new national union had started up, and some of the Knights of Labor left to become members of the new group.

Do Detective Work

HISTORIANS USE artifacts—such as photographs—to learn about the past. They ask many questions and look very closely for answers. They look for answers to these questions: who, what, when, why, where. Sometimes they find answers to all their questions.

Use your skills as a historian to analyze this historic photo. Can you answer any of the five Ws? Write statements that are absolute facts. Write statements that may be facts. Write questions you continue to have about the photo.

WHO	WHAT	WHEN	WHY	WHERE

Working girls.

Courtesy of the Library of Congress, Prints & Photographs Division, LC-USZ62-65668

Who: Young female factory workers.

What: Spoolers in textile mills operated machines that combined threads from 10 to 15 bobbins to form yarn.

When: October 1908

Why: Many products were made in American factories during the 1800s. Textile manufacturing was a big business. Young women often worked in the mills. They helped support their families with their wages.

Where: Lincoln Cotton Mill in Evansville, Indiana

Samuel Gompers was only 14 years old when he joined the Cigar Makers' International Union of America in New York. His time as a member of this union gave him skills and experiences that led him to start one of the biggest labor organizations in American history when he was 36 years of age. Samuel and another cigar maker, Adolph Strasser, started the American Federation of Labor (AFL) in 1886. Like the Knights of Labor, the AFL planned to become a national organization. It was different than the Knights of Labor in other ways. The AFL was an organization of several different craft unions—cigar makers, carpenters, mineworkers, steelworkers, and others. Only people with special skills in these crafts could join. Blacks and women were not welcome. By 1900 the union had a membership of almost 1 million.

All those people joined the AFL because they faced unfair situations at their workplaces. They were required to work longer days for less pay when hard economic times hit businesses. They were fired when business owners needed to cut expenses. When a worker was injured on the job, he often had to pay his own medical bills, and he lost his wages while he was unable to work. Sometimes, if an injured worker took too long to recover, he was replaced. Workers who joined the AFL were hopeful that the union could make a difference. The AFL promised to help members get better wages, shorter days, and medical benefits.

The AFL leaders wanted to use a strategy called *collective bargaining* to reach its goals for workers. They believed in negotiating or bargaining with business owners to solve problems. But if talking didn't work, the union members knew they had to do something that would draw attention to their troubles. One way to do this was to strike—to refuse to work until they got what they wanted. Sometimes it worked; other times it didn't.

Strike!

WORKERS WHO wanted change had tried strikes long before the AFL existed. One of the earliest strikes of the Industrial Revolution took place in a textile mill in Lowell, Massachusetts, in 1836. Harriet Hanson, an 11-year-old girl who worked at the mill, led other workers in the strike, which was called a *turn out*. The mill owners had cut wages and decided to stop paying the girls' rent at their boardinghouses. Harriet watched as mill hands began to walk out of the factory. When none of the girls in her area moved, she said, "I don't care what you do, I am going to turn out, whether anyone else does or not." The others followed.

Sarah Wilson led a strike of factory workers in Lewiston, Maine, in 1854. They were expected to work 14 hours for a day's pay. Sarah and her fellow factory workers refused to return to work until the workday was reduced to 11 hours. They marched to a meeting hall where Sarah spoke to the crowd: "If we worked only 11 hours, we should have some time to improve our minds, but as it is we work 14 hours and are tied to the mill."

The *New York Times* described a strike of thousands of shoe and textile workers in Massachusetts in February 1860. As the striking men and women marched through the streets they carried signs: OUR BOSSES GRIND US; DOWN WITH TYRANNY; NO SYMPATHY WITH THE RICH.

Twenty black women who washed and ironed clothes for hire in Atlanta, Georgia, in 1881 formed a union called the Washing

Striking women in a garment factory in New York City in 1909.

Striking messenger boys in New York City in November 1916.

Society. Before long, 3,000 women had joined. They went on strike for better wages. The women wanted $1 for every 12 pounds of washing. The striking washing women were successful in gaining better wages.

Eleven-year-old Moses Burns and 13-year-old John Alleppo led a strike of newsboys in New York City in the summer of 1899. About 300 newsies joined the strike. Those who didn't were beaten with sticks by the two strike leaders, whom the police called "perfect demons." Police managed to grab them and haul them into the police station, where they were charged with disorderly conduct.

Over the early years of the Industrial Revolution small, local strikes like these had mixed results. They involved only a small number of people. And business owners often denied strikers better conditions. But more widespread strikes had greater impact. In the late 1800s massive strikes by workers across whole regions of the country captured the nation's attention.

The Great Railroad Strike of 1877

THE ZEPP family of Martinsburg, West Virginia, had worked for the Baltimore and Ohio Railroad for two generations. Henry made about $360 per year as an engineer in the 1840s. By 1877 his sons, Richard and George, were working for the company. That was the year they became involved in one of the biggest labor strikes of the time.

The owners of the Baltimore and Ohio Railroad, one of the largest railroads in the country, had been affected by the poor economy. They weren't making as much money as in the past. They decided to reduce workers' wages—twice within eight months. That was a severe hardship for many, including the Zepp family.

The rail workers decided they wouldn't work until their wages were restored. On July 16 a crew refused to operate a car loaded with cattle heading to market from Martinsburg. It was the start of something big.

Over the next week, rail freight cars were at a standstill along the Baltimore and Ohio line and other lines as workers in several states—Pennsylvania, Ohio, Illinois, Maryland, and others—refused to work. They had been affected by wage cuts too. Local militias were called out to control the crowds of strikers and people who supported their cause. President Rutherford B. Hayes sent federal troops to some places to control the situation. The railroad owners tried to get non-strikers to run the trains.

In Martinsburg, George Zepp did not support the strike. He continued to go to work at the rail yard every day. He carried a gun, waving it over his head to warn off attacking strikers. His mother, Julie, didn't approve of his behavior. A newspaper reporter described Mrs. Zepp chasing her son down the street with a broom. And while George and Julie made their way through the wild crowds of strikers, the police were arresting the other Zepp brother, Richard. They accused him of leading the unruly strikers.

By the time it was all over in early August, 100,000 workers had gone on strike. At least a thousand people—like Richard Zepp—had been arrested. Thousands of dollars of property had been damaged. Hundreds of strikers, militia, and innocent bystanders—including children—in several states had been injured or killed.

Great Railroad Strike of 1877.

LUCY PARSONS

Lucy Parsons was born a slave. She was never sure of her birth year, but she thought it was around 1853. She wasn't certain about who her parents, grandparents, and great-grandparents were. She thought she was part African American, Mexican, and Native American.

Although Lucy was uncertain of her past, she knew what she wanted for the future. She wanted to live in an America where there were no poor and homeless people—where hardworking people could earn a fair wage and have some time to enjoy life.

When Lucy left slavery behind and married Albert Parsons, the two moved from Texas to Chicago, Illinois, in 1873. The Parsonses wanted to make Americans aware of the poor and homeless in America. They wrote articles and made speeches about the vast differences between the rich and poor. They worked to make the lives of workers better. The Parsonses were very active in the Knights of Labor. But they were disappointed when conditions continued to get worse for working men and women. They began to make speeches calling for more radical activities to bring attention to the hardships of many Americans.

The Parsonses had helped organize the workers at the McCormick Harvesting Machine Company. They brought their children, Albert Jr. and Lulu, to Haymarket Square after strikers were killed by police. Albert Sr. was one of the speakers. He was one of the men charged with causing the riot. He was given the death sentence and hanged.

Lucy promised her husband before his hanging that she would continue to do the work they had started together. She spent the rest of her life trying to make the lives of America's workers better.

The Great Railroad Strike of 1877 was a widespread event that affected people across several states. After the strikes ended, most workers agreed they hadn't gained much. Only a few workers saw their wages restored. But the workers learned lessons. They began to realize that to be successful they needed a strong nationwide system of unions to help coordinate their efforts.

The Haymarket Riot

A STRIKE at the McCormick Harvesting Machine Company in Chicago, Illinois, turned out very badly in May 1886. The problems started when a group refused to work until the company owners agreed to an eight-hour day. When the police were brought in to handle a crowd outside the factory, some strikers were killed and injured. The next day a large group of workers gathered at a place called Haymarket Square. They were listening to speakers talking about unfair conditions in factories. The police came. Someone—it was never proven who—dropped a bomb in the midst of the police. They responded by shooting into the crowd. Police officers and strikers were killed.

Eight men were arrested. They were charged, tried, and found guilty of starting a riot. Five were given the death sentence and were scheduled for execution. One committed suicide in prison before the execution. The other four were hanged. Three other men received prison sentences but were later released from prison. In 1893 the governor of Illinois granted them pardons. He said they had not been given a fair trial.

Steelworkers' Strike at Homestead

"HEAR THE orphans tell their sad story / Father was killed by the Pinkerton men." The words of a popular song by William W. Delaney in 1892 told the tragic story of a strike by steelworkers at a mill in Homestead, Pennsylvania.

Drawing of the Haymarket Riot.
Courtesy of the Library of Congress, Prints & Photographs Division, LC-USZ62-796

The mill was owned by Andrew Carnegie, who was vacationing at a castle in Scotland when the workers decided to strike. But the manager, Henry Frick, took control of the situation.

The Amalgamated Association of Iron and Steel Workers union was trying to discuss wages and working conditions with Frick. He didn't like labor unions. After a short time, Frick refused to talk to the union. He closed the mill, and the workers couldn't work. Frick thought the men would leave the union and work for the wages he offered. But Frick was wrong.

When 3,000 steelworkers refused to work, the manager hired the Pinkerton National Detective Agency to protect *strikebreakers*, new workers he had brought to the mill to replace the striking employees. In the middle of the night on July 5, boatloads of detectives pulled up to the banks of the Monongahela River. They carried guns and were ready to use them. The strikers and other townspeople—including children—left their beds and ran to the river to stop the detectives.

Tempers were hot. The detectives used their rifles, and the strikers fought with guns and dynamite. The two sides battled for 14 hours. When the gunfire ended, there were dead and wounded on both sides.

It was the beginning of several months of trouble at Homestead. Striking workers—and

Homestead Strike in Pennsylvania. Steelworkers and townspeople battle with Pinkertons, 1892.

Courtesy of the Library of Congress, Prints & Photographs Division, LC-USZ61-984

their wives and children—attacked strikebreakers with bricks, stones, and lumps of coal when they tried to enter the mill. Someone used dynamite to damage a house where strikebreakers lived. The governor sent the National Guard to control strikers and protect strikebreakers. Major General George Snowden described the situation: "It reminds me of a seething volcano ready to burst forth at any moment."

As the strike dragged on for weeks, many people suffered. Families who lived in the mill's company housing had to leave their homes. Businesses lost money because striking families couldn't buy goods.

Some workers couldn't hold out, so they went back to work. But that could be dangerous for family members. Sherriff's deputies were called to guard a teacher at the Third Ward Public School. Her dad had gone back to work, and she had been threatened by students.

The strike didn't last long. By November many of the workers had returned to the mill. The union had been crushed. Men who went back gave in to Frick and Carnegie. They worked for lower wages, and their workday was 12 hours long. The Homestead Strike was viewed as a failure for workers.

The Pullman Strike

PEOPLE WHO worked for the Pullman Palace Car Factory near Chicago, Illinois, in 1894 were lucky in some ways. They had jobs building luxury railroad sleeper cars. They lived in houses provided by the company. They shopped in stores run by the company. But they weren't happy.

The economy was very bad throughout the United States. George Pullman, the owner of the company, had laid off workers. He cut the pay for those who remained. And those company houses—the workers were *forced* to live in them. For rent, they had to pay whatever amount the company demanded. The rent was subtracted from their pay. When their wages were cut, the workers thought their rent should be reduced too. But George Pullman disagreed. When a group of workers asked the company to cut the rent, they were fired. George Pullman and his family left town for their New Jersey cottage called Fairlawn, with a view of the Atlantic Ocean.

In May, workers decided to strike, and they asked the American Railway Union (ARU) members to join them. The union members agreed. They started a boycott of any railroad company that used Pullman sleeping cars. About 2,000 Pullman sleepers were on trains across the country.

Many trains were at a standstill. US mail was not delivered. Federal troops arrived in the Chicago area to help get trains moving. The situation became deadly in July when strikers became violent. They set fire to railcars, blocked tracks, and attacked rail workers who weren't boycotting. The troops fired shots into the crowds of strikers. Some were killed.

By August the strike was over. The ARU disbanded. Strikers who went back to their old jobs had to promise never to join a union. Their pay was the same as before the strike.

The rents on the company houses stayed the same.

Success

FIRES, EXPLOSIONS, and collapsing buildings. Men, women, and children faced all these dangers in addition to low wages and long hours when they went to work in the 1800s. During the Industrial Revolution workers decided to do something about these problems. They started unions to ask for better conditions. They refused to work until business owners treated them fairly. They went on strike. Sometimes unions and strikes *did* make life better for workers, but not always. It took many years of struggles by ordinary people to see success. Gradually, building on past successes, America's workers brought about change.

6

HELP AND HOPE FOR BETTER LIVES

I**N THE SPRING OF** **1895,** 14-year-old Arthur Howe and George Brown decided they couldn't bear another day of spankings and prayers at the Howard Orphan Asylum in Brooklyn, New York. One evening they managed to get their hands on a crowbar and started whacking away at the walls of their dormitory—planning to make their escape. When they were caught in the act, they were thrown in a room under lock and key. The next morning they were taken before a judge who threatened to send them to a *house of refuge*, a facility for delinquent kids. It was supposed to scare the boys. But they said any place was better than the orphan asylum.

"They spank us and then pray for us at all hours of the day. The prayers are too long and the spankings are too hard," Arthur said.

Arthur and George were like many people living during the Industrial Revolution. They were just trying to survive from day to day in a fast-changing world. They were dependent on others to provide them with the necessities of life. And they were looking for a better situation—one that would give them a brighter future. While there were those who offered help in various ways, it wasn't always what it seemed. However, reformers—who became known as *Progressives* in the late 1800s—did actually make a difference.

Orphans' asylum in Nebraska, 1897.
Courtesy of the Library of Congress, Prints & Photographs Division, LC-USZ62-53535

Urchins and Orphans

WHEN ARTHUR Howe and George Brown tried to break out of the Howard Orphan Asylum in 1895, they may have had good reasons for doing so. Orphanages, or orphan asylums, were often dreary and dangerous places. At the time there were an estimated 100,000 children living in 1,000 orphanages in New York City alone. There were thousands of kids living on the streets, sleeping in doorways, and, in some cases, stealing food to survive. These children of the streets were called *street urchins*. Other large cities, such as Philadelphia, Boston, and Chicago, had large numbers of orphans and urchins too.

For those who were lucky—or unlucky—enough to live in an orphanage, life could be harsher than on the streets. All the kids, or inmates, slept together in dormitories—as many as 50 or 60 to a room. Older inmates were sometimes mean to younger kids. Everyone had chores: sweeping, cleaning, laundry, or kitchen work. Orphanages usually offered vocational training so when inmates left they had some hope of getting a job. Boys were taught a trade: shoemaking, carpentry, or farming practices. Girls learned skills to help them get jobs as maids.

Orphanages seemed to be short of everything—food, clothing, and, most important, loving attention by caring adults. Not all adults who worked at orphanages were bad, but there was plenty of room for improvement. There was very little regulation of orphans' care by the government in the early 1800s. So if the adults who operated the orphanages were cruel or wicked, they could get away with treating the orphans badly.

Kids went to orphanages for a variety of reasons. It wasn't always because both parents were dead. Sometimes the parents were too poor or sick to care for their kids. A single father or mother struggled to work *and* care for children, and there were few day care programs. Some parents were drug addicts or alcoholics or were in jail. An orphanage might have been the only option.

Most orphanages were not meant to be permanent homes for kids. At age 14 kids were expected to leave and find work. In some cases that meant becoming *indentured*. In other words, the orphan went to work at a home or business for no pay. Their room and meals were considered payment. After a certain time, they were free to leave. But they usually spent many years in indenture.

As bad as some orphanages were, they were considered an improvement in the care of helpless kids. During the 1700s parentless kids were put in places called *almshouses* or *poorhouses*—with adult inmates. And those

All About Gruel

MMMM, GRUEL. Meals at orphanages were extremely bad. A typical menu looked something like this:

Breakfast: coffee, bread, and maybe a little butter

Lunch: watery stew and a hard hunk of bread

Supper: tea and bread with a spoonful of molasses

An especially unappetizing alternative to watery stew was a dish called *gruel*. There were variations on this dish, but orphanage cooks usually followed a similar recipe, boiling a cereal grain like oats, wheat, or rye in milk or water using a coal-powered cookstove.

If you're feeling very brave, follow this recipe to make your own gruel.

Adult supervision required

YOU'LL NEED
- Microwave-safe bowl
- ¼ cup of quick oatmeal
- 2 cups of water
- A pinch of salt
- Microwave
- Hot pads

Combine the oatmeal and the water in the bowl. Toss in a tiny bit of salt. Cook in the microwave for one to two minutes. Use hot pads to carefully remove the hot gruel from the microwave.

Warning: Gruel is watery and tasteless. Now you know what orphans of the Industrial Revolution had to endure!

But oatmeal *can* be quite tasty. For a tastier version of gruel, try this:

YOU'LL NEED
- Microwave-safe bowl
- ¼ cup of quick oatmeal
- ½ cup of milk
- Microwave
- Hot pads
- Dried fruit and nuts

Combine the oatmeal and the milk in the bowl. Cook in the microwave for one to two minutes. Use hot pads to carefully remove the bowl from the microwave. Sprinkle dried fruit and nuts over the oatmeal, or add other tasty treats.

Enjoy!

adults were sometimes dangerously mentally ill or even criminal. In the early 1800s reformers began to realize that kids should live in separate facilities. So throughout the 19th century thousands of orphanages were started all across the country. And they were bursting at the seams during the Industrial Revolution.

Juvenile delinquents learning the shoemaking trade.

Care for Troublemakers

TEN-YEAR-OLD HARRY and 14-year-old Benjamin lived in Harlem, New York, with their parents in 1894. But they were very unhappy living at home, so they decided to run away one day in February. They didn't get far when the police caught up with them. They were brought before a judge, who threatened them with confinement in the New York House of Refuge.

"Do you want to go where you'll have nothing to eat but bread and water, and where you'll have to go to bed at 5 o'clock every night and be locked in a room?" the judge asked the boys.

"Yes!" both boys responded in unison.

Harry and Benjamin said that at their home they were beat and kicked by their big brother. Their dad was not helpful in defending the smaller boys. He said they were *incorrigible*, or not able to be helped or controlled.

But the judge had mercy and sent them back home, promising to send them to the house of refuge if he saw them again.

Harry and Benjamin were probably badly mistaken if they thought life at the house of refuge would be better than their situation at home. Houses of refuge housed homeless kids and those who had committed crimes. Sometimes parents put their kids in a house of refuge if they couldn't handle them. Some houses of refuge were run like a military camp. The kids wore uniforms and marched to meals. Everyone went to bed at the same time. The keepers, or caretakers, sometimes beat the kids with straps. Rowdy kids were locked away by themselves.

The day was full for the inmates of a house of refuge. School classes took place for a short time early in the morning and again later in the day. The kids spent most of the day working—making shoes, socks, baskets, and rat traps. They didn't keep the money they made. It was used to buy food, clothing, and heat for the dormitories.

Reform schools were another option for unruly kids during the years of the Industrial Revolution. They were all about reforming—or improving—kids' behavior so they would become respectable adults. Reform schools were generally a little different than houses of refuge. They also were run in a military style, but the kids spent most of their day in school rather than working. The goal was to help kids who were in trouble learn a skill so they could leave the school prepared to earn a living. The kids would be reformed, or changed, by the time they left.

Reform schools were meant to be more like a family situation. There was a patron or matron (father or mother) in charge of about 40

Weave a Placemat

TROUBLED KIDS living at houses of refuge spent a good deal of their time working. School was not a priority. Kids' jobs were important because they brought in money to help run the institution. They worked at a variety of jobs. Many house of refuge kids learned basket making. Test your weaving skills by making a placemat.

YOU'LL NEED
- Ruler
- Scissors
- Card stock or stiff paper (you could use waterproof paper so you can wipe food messes off the placemat, or use fabric that can be cleaned)
- Glue stick or tape

Cut nine strips of paper 1 foot long by 1 inch wide. Then cut nine strips of paper 9 inches long by 1 inch wide.

Lay out the long strips at a horizontal angle. Begin to weave the shorter strips through the longer ones at a vertical angle. Line up the beginning edge. Glue or tape the beginning pieces together to keep the weave secure.

Continue weaving until all the strips have been used. Trim uneven edges, and glue or tape the ending strips.

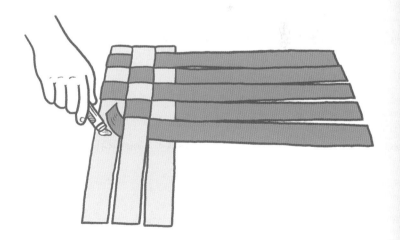

89

kids. The residents lived in "cottages" rather than huge, institution-like buildings. The patrons and matrons were supposed to use *corrective discipline.* That meant they did not use whipping and hitting to change the kids' behavior.

The idea of reform schools spread across the United States during the last half of the 1800s. Some people thought they were better for kids than houses of refuge. But, as with houses of refuge, not all reform schools were the same. The kids were at the mercy of the caretakers. Some were caring; others were not.

Improving the Lives of Orphans and Juveniles

ORPHANAGES, REFORM schools, and 14-hour days at the factory made life tough for a kid during the Industrial Revolution. But some compassionate adults saw the crushing problems these kids faced and knew they had to do something to help. Gradually, these individuals and groups brought about changes.

Throughout the 1800s and into the 1900s, adults had a variety of ideas about how to deal with homeless, troubled, and working kids. They convinced government leaders to provide money to make children's lives better. Because of their work, laws were passed to protect kids.

Most agreed that it was a good idea to separate orphans and troubled kids from adults in institutions. That's why so many orphanages and reform schools were started. As the 1800s progressed, some individuals who were concerned about the welfare of children began to think, study, and talk about different ways to help children in need. By the early 1900s more and more child welfare reformers believed that orphanages should be closed. They also were very critical of the idea of "placing out" kids. They criticized agencies like the Children's Aid Society, which sent New York kids on orphan trains to live with families far from their homes.

Amos Warner had managed charities in Maryland and Washington, DC, in the mid-1800s. He studied the lives of poor people and was greatly respected. When he wrote in 1875 that orphanages were not good places to raise kids, others listened. Amos and other child welfare reformers tried to convince people that orphans should be raised in family situations—not institutions. He believed that kids without parents should go to foster families.

Homer Folks was another child welfare expert in the late 1800s. He believed kids should stay with their parents if at all possible—even if a family was struggling. In families where parents couldn't care for their kids, he said, foster families were better than orphanages.

Homer pushed for training for people who worked with homeless and troubled kids. This idea was new. Most child care workers in orphanages and houses of refuge were uneducated. Homer wanted government agencies to be more involved in child welfare issues.

Reformers began to realize that a system for dealing with child welfare issues needed to be in place in the United States. Some states, counties, and cities had groups that looked out for kids. But it was hit-or-miss. Reformers wanted more help for kids, wherever they lived. During the last part of the 1800s and early 1900s, reformers made progress. But sometimes help for kids came in unusual ways.

Henry Bergh was sickened by the way animals were treated, so he decided to do something about it. In 1866 he formed the American Society for the Prevention of Cruelty to Animals (ASPCA) in New York. Over the next 22 years, similar groups were operating in most states. Henry and others worked to get laws passed to protect animals. Henry's concern for the welfare of animals led some people to turn to him when looking for help for humans.

In 1874 Etta Wheeler, a New York church worker who helped poor tenement families, heard about a little orphan girl named Mary Ellen. Neighbors told Etta that Mary Ellen's foster family was abusing her. Etta visited the family and saw for herself the abuse suffered by the little girl. When Etta had a hard time getting help for Mary Ellen, she turned to Henry Bergh. Because he had done so much to help animals, Etta thought he might help with this little orphan girl.

Etta was right. Henry asked the lawyer of the ASPCA to help prosecute Mary Ellen's foster mother in court. They were successful. Mary Ellen was rescued from a terrible home. Her foster mother went to jail.

Henry's involvement with Mary Ellen's case led him to do something for humans—just as he had for animals. He started the New York Society for the Prevention of Cruelty to Children in 1874. Over the next few years, similar societies began around the country.

As the problems brought about by the Industrial Revolution continued, more and more kids found themselves in trouble with the law. Parents were busy and tired from working 14 to 16 hours a day in factories, sweatshops, or mines. Kids were alone for long periods of time. School attendance wasn't required or enforced. Some kids couldn't keep out of trouble. They ended up before judges and were sentenced to houses of refuge or reform schools. Concerned adults took actions to bring about changes. They wanted to give hope to troubled kids.

Tell a Story with Photographs

PHOTOGRAPHERS LIKE Lewis Hine and Jacob Riis used their cameras to tell stories about the people of the Industrial Revolution. Their work helped future generations understand the past.

Think about kids' lives today. What activities and objects represent a typical kid's life?

YOU'LL NEED
- ➤ Camera
- ➤ Poster board
- ➤ Tape or glue stick
- ➤ Marker

Take pictures of kids doing everyday activities (for example, playing outside, riding a bike, dancing, cooking, playing sports, doing chores). Photograph objects that will help future generations understand your way of life.

Collect the photographs and display them on a poster board (either electronic or actual). Include captions with each picture that explain the photograph. Try to imagine a person seeing your display 100 years from now.

During the last part of the 1800s changes did occur. Reformers who became known as *child savers* worked to improve services for young offenders. The child saving movement was begun mostly by middle- and upper-class women who believed it was their duty to save delinquent children. Child savers could be found all over the United States, but a group in Chicago brought about a big change. In 1899 the child savers of the Chicago Women's Club got the Illinois legislature to set up a juvenile court system. Offenders under the age of 18 would have special consideration by the courts. Judges had more flexibility in dealing with the offenders. And special programs were set up to help young offenders. The Illinois law was the first to set up a completely separate system of courts for young offenders. Other states followed the Illinois model.

Improving the Lives of Working Kids

AS THE Industrial Revolution continued into the early 1900s, many kids were working in factories and mines. In 1890 1.5 million kids were working in industrial jobs. The number grew to 2 million by 1910.

Plenty of people were unhappy about kids working so hard. One individual who decided to do something about child labor was—not a surprise—a teacher. In the early 1900s, Lewis Hine taught at a school in New York City. He took his students on a field trip to photograph newly arriving immigrants entering the United States at Ellis Island. This was the start of a new career. Lewis quit teaching and became a photographer. He spent the next years taking photographs of kids all over the country as they worked in factories, mines, and meatpacking plants. His disturbing photos captured the attention of many Americans. Over the years Lewis's photographs helped to bring about laws against child labor.

When Florence Kelley was a child, her father took her to see kids working in factories. Those experiences stayed with Florence. When she was an adult living in Chicago in the late 1800s, Florence started visiting factories and meatpacking plants to observe kids at work. She didn't like what she saw. She started to collect data and used her information to bring change to Illinois laws. It worked. Illinois passed legislation that kept kids under 14 out of factories. Florence was hired by the state to inspect factories to make certain the law wasn't being violated. She spent the rest of her life working to end child labor and to make the workplace better for adults.

People like Lewis and Florence worked for years to call attention to child welfare problems brought about by the Industrial Revolution. Reformers from every state saw similar situations. Many believed something needed to be done at the national level.

Progress was made in 1909. Child welfare reformers managed to get President Theodore Roosevelt interested in their cause. He agreed to sponsor a meeting in Washington, DC. The White House Conference on Children and Youth brought together people from all over the United States. It was the first time a national conference on the welfare of kids was held.

Another big step was taken in 1912 when the Children's Bureau was set up. It was an agency of the federal government. Members of the bureau—people who worked for the government—would investigate and report on children from across the United States. Finally, in 1916, the US Congress passed a law to protect kids. The new law said kids under age 14 could not work in factories and shops. It took many more years for Congress to outlaw child labor. That happened in 1938, when the Fair Labor Standards Act said kids under 16 couldn't work in most jobs.

Those with Little Hope

IT MIGHT be difficult to feel hopeful if you were living in a place called the *home for the friendless.* But for the people who needed the services offered by the homes for the friendless, the name didn't matter. They were men, women, and children who had nowhere to go. They may not have been friendless, but they were usually homeless.

There were homes for the friendless all over the country. Some welcomed only women and children. Others were open to men and women. Some cared for the elderly or the sick. Many were started by concerned citizens who

This home for the friendless was established in 1874 for women and children in Dubuque, Iowa.
Frank Buol Collection, Loras College Center for Dubuque History

saw a need in their communities and decided to do something to help those who felt hopeless—and friendless.

Most towns and cities during the Industrial Revolution had leaders and activists who noticed the poor and helpless. These caring individuals brought others together to provide food, clothes, shelter, and heat for the needy. They set up homes for the friendless and other resources for the less fortunate. This was especially true during hard economic times.

Although the Industrial Revolution brought opportunities for work, it also brought uncertainty. During bad economic times, factories and mines closed. Railroads failed. Workers went on strike for better wages, but often they weren't successful. People lost their jobs. And the government didn't help the unemployed. They were on their own.

During the late 1800s the economy was very uncertain. Things were especially bad at two different times—1873 and 1893. These periods became known as the Panic of 1873 and the Panic of 1893. Business owners and workers were frightened. And they should have been, because they were in for some terrible times.

Many businesses failed during the Panic of 1873. Three million workers lost their jobs. Workers in piano factories, sugar refineries, book binderies, paper factories, and hat factories saw their wages reduced or jobs eliminated. The bad economy lasted for about five

A man begging on the streets of New York City.

Courtesy of the Library of Congress, Prints & Photographs Division, LC-DIG-ggbain-00095 years. The *New York Times* reported in 1874 that "men and women who would die sooner than beg were compelled to seek relief to prevent their children from starving."

The Panic of 1893 was just as bad. By the end of that year, over 15,000 businesses had failed. Even banks closed. Three million people were out of work again.

During these times many families were hurting. A woman who worked to help the unemployed said, "It has seemed to us sometimes that the whole world was unemployed." Individuals and groups stepped up to help the less fortunate.

In New York City in 1873 coal—necessary for heating and cooking—was made available at drastically reduced prices to poor families. *Soup kitchens* were set up in cities to provide food to the needy. Officials in Boston reported they had supplied meals to over 10,000 families in one month during the winter of 1875. The city of Taunton, Massachusetts, loaned money to unemployed men; their names were added to a list. When the city had work that needed to be done, the men would be asked to "work off" their loans.

In 1894 the New York City government funded a program that hired out-of-work men to build sidewalks, repair streets, and complete landscaping work in the city parks. A church asked members to donate money to

hire unemployed men to sweep the streets in the neighborhood surrounding the church property. When men and women from some cigar-making factories were out of work because of the lagging economy, a charitable group started a restaurant in the neighborhood. They sold carry-out meals to poor and out-of-work families. For five cents the families got a quart of stew, coffee, and bread.

Many of the poor and unemployed in the large cities of the Industrial Revolution were immigrants. They had an especially difficult time partly because they were far from their homelands. Some had left their families to

People who had nowhere to stay could rent a room for a night in a lodging house. These men were relaxing in a New York City lodging house in 1908 or 1909.

Courtesy of the Library of Congress, Prints & Photographs Division, LC-USZ62-72456

SAVIOR OR SCAMMER?

A bit of mystery surrounded Clementine Lamadrid. In 1887 she set up her first St. Andrew's One-Cent Coffee Stand on a street corner in New York City. For one cent per item, poor people could purchase a hearty meal every day. Carry-out was also available. Customers chose from a menu of coffee, bread, beef stew, vegetables, pork and beans, or fish cakes.

Clementine said she was married to a wealthy importer and that the couple would contribute their own money to help pay for the meals. She personally visited food suppliers and got their lowest prices. She talked restaurants into donating their unused bread at the end of the day. After a while Clementine started asking wealthy people to give money to her for the stands. She persuaded musicians to give concerts at places like Carnegie Hall. She said the profits went to her coffee stands—allowing her to open more stands on more corners.

Some other charitable groups began to ask questions about Clementine's activities. Newspapers reported that the Lamadrids lived a luxurious lifestyle in a beautiful apartment—and that Joaquin Maria Lamadrid was not an importer at all. In fact, some believed the couple's wealth came from Clementine's one-cent stands.

Did she take most of the money for herself that wealthy people donated to the cause? It's a mystery of history that may never be solved. But even after Clementine died in 1908, her husband continued to get wealthy people to make contributions to the St. Andrew's One-Cent Coffee Stands "in her memory." Whether or not the Lamadrids were scammers, many poor New Yorkers were grateful for the cheap, healthy meals they purchased at the stands.

Men having coffee at a One-Cent Coffee Stand.

Courtesy of the Library of Congress, Prints & Photographs Division, LC-DIG-ggbain-01037

RIGHT: **St. Andrew's One-Cent Coffee Stand menu. The stands operated on street corners where anyone could purchase a healthy meal for a few cents.**

Courtesy of the Library of Congress, American Memory Collection, RBPE 13400300

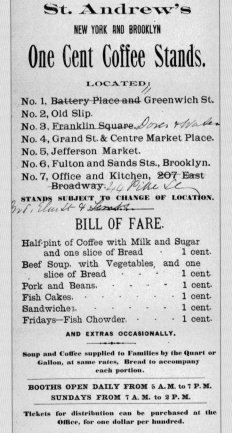

St. Andrew's

NEW YORK AND BROOKLYN

One Cent Coffee Stands.

LOCATED:

No. 1, Battery Place and Greenwich St.
No. 2, Old Slip.
No. 3, Franklin Square.
No. 4, Grand St. & Centre Market Place.
No. 5, Jefferson Market.
No. 6, Fulton and Sands Sts., Brooklyn.
No. 7, Office and Kitchen, 207 East Broadway.

STANDS SUBJECT TO CHANGE OF LOCATION.

BILL OF FARE.

Half-pint of Coffee with Milk and Sugar and one slice of Bread · 1 cent.
Beef Soup, with Vegetables, and one slice of Bread · · 1 cent.
Pork and Beans, · · · · 1 cent.
Fish Cakes, · · · · · 1 cent.
Sandwiches, · · · · · 1 cent.
Fridays—Fish Chowder, · · · 1 cent.

AND EXTRAS OCCASIONALLY.

Soup and Coffee supplied to Families by the Quart or Gallon, at same rates, Bread to accompany each portion.

BOOTHS OPEN DAILY FROM 5 A.M. to 7 P.M.
SUNDAYS FROM 7 A.M. to 2 P.M.

Tickets for distribution can be purchased at the Office, for one dollar per hundred.

come to America for opportunities. Many couldn't speak English.

It didn't help when people blamed immigrants for all the problems of the time—including diseases, high unemployment, and low wages. Some Americans believed all immigrants were troublemakers or criminals. In some cases, relief agencies refused to help people who weren't US citizens.

However, immigrants did find welcoming surroundings at *settlement houses*. These were places located in poor neighborhoods, where residents could come together as a community to learn and have fun. Settlement houses offered child care, literacy classes, health services, training in job skills, as well as art, theater, and music classes.

A man named Stanton Coit opened the first US settlement house, called Neighborhood Guild, in 1886 in New York City. Located in a very poor section of the city, it later became known as University Settlement. This settlement offered kindergarten and adult education classes, a library, a swimming pool and gymnasium, as well as dance lessons.

Settlement houses were often run by wealthy or middle-class women who wanted to help the poor. They volunteered their time. They lived at the settlement houses. Some settlement houses were tied to religious groups; others were not.

Italian, Irish, German, Greek, Russian, and Polish immigrants found friendly faces at a settlement house in Chicago, where Jane Addams and Ellen Gates Starr started Hull House in 1889. In Boston many Italian, Syrian, and Greek

IMMIGRANT PHOTOGRAPHER

Jacob Riis knew what it was like to be an immigrant in New York City in 1870. He had come to America from Denmark. At times, he had to beg for food. Jacob missed his homeland. But most of all, he was sad because the girl he wanted to marry refused him. Elizabeth Giortz stayed in Denmark when Jacob left for America.

Jacob worked at dead-end jobs for years. Then, in 1877 he got a job as a reporter. This led him to some of the poorest parts of the city. He took a camera as he walked the streets. His photography made him a celebrity. All over the country people saw Jacob's photos of the tenements, factories, and slums of America.

In 1890 Jacob wrote *How the Other Half Lives*. It was a book packed with shocking photos of life in the slums. Over the next 20 years Jacob wrote about the lives of the poor. He traveled across the country giving speeches and showing his photos.

Jacob Riis became a greatly admired man. He became friends with President Theodore Roosevelt. Millions of Americans saw the greatness in him. But it was the admiration of one person that Jacob cherished most in his life.

Six years after he moved to America, Jacob finally won the heart of his true love back in Denmark. Elizabeth Giortz had changed her mind. She sent a letter to Jacob in New York. "You are good and strong.... I will give you my hand in marriage," she wrote. Jacob and Elizabeth were married in 1876. Elizabeth had finally seen in Jacob what millions of Americans saw—a good and strong man.

Try to Understand an Unfamiliar Language

WHEN IMMIGRANTS arrived in the United States during the Industrial Revolution they often did not understand English. They could not read or write English either. Have you ever been in a situation where you did not understand what people were saying?

YOU'LL NEED

➤ Pencil and paper
➤ Computer with Internet access

It is 1899. Antonio has just arrived in America from Italy. He does not speak English. He meets you on the street and says this to you:

Dove si trova la fabbrica di scarpe? Devo affrettarmi. Questo è il primo giorno al mio nuovo lavoro. Sono in ritardo per il lavoro. Il mio capo mi licenzierà se arrivo tardi. Non capisco le vostre indicazioni. Mi sono perso. Puoi aiutarmi? Puoi aiutarmi?

You do not understand Italian. But you can tell from Antonio's voice and actions that he is very worried.

Read Antonio's statement aloud. Do you recognize any of the words? Which ones look familiar? Write down the words that you think you may know. And write down what you think they mean. How do you feel when you can't understand Antonio's words?

In the 1800s no one had the Internet. But you are lucky. You can get help by using a free online translation tool. Use one to translate Antonio's statement to English.

immigrants gathered at Denison House. It was established by Emily Greene Balch, Helen Cheever, and Vida Scudder in 1892. These women were disturbed by the gaps they saw between the rich and poor in America. They hoped to help bridge the gap. Dr. Jane Robbins was called "the angel of the tenements" for the work she did through a settlement called the College Settlement House in New York City.

By 1900 there were 100 settlement houses across America. At one point the number rose to 400. Each was a little different because the idea was for community members to influence and shape the nature of each house. But all settlement houses were built around some basic beliefs and practices. They all tried to offer a place for friendship and education. They all tried to offer help and hope to communities that were in desperate need of both.

Making Conditions Better

THE YEARS of the Industrial Revolution were very good years for some. But the revolutionary changes in the way people lived led to hardships for many. Cities were not ready to deal with the rush of newcomers. Many of the people were not prepared for the lives they would find in the cities. Some parents couldn't support their families on low wages and high rents. Workers' strikes and uncertain economic times took a toll on many families. People got sick. Kids suffered too. Some were abandoned by their parents. Many men, women, and children needed help. There was never enough help for all those who were in distress. And sometimes the people who offered help were uncaring, deceitful, or cruel.

Many caring and concerned individuals saw the misery and tried to help. As a group, they became known as the Progressives. And their actions were called the Progressive Movement. They began to understand more about problems brought about by industrialization. Universities offered courses for students who wanted to help people with problems. This was the beginning of the social work profession. The Progressive reformers of the Industrial Revolution took steps to improve people's lives. Gradually, their ideas and work resulted in change. Laws were passed to protect adults and kids. Organizations were set up to serve people in need. As the Industrial Revolution moved into the 20th century, help and hope seemed to follow.

This orchestra was an example of cultural and educational opportunities offered by settlement houses in large cities.

Courtesy of the Library of Congress, Prints & Photographs Division, LC-B2-3849-6

7

A NEW CULTURE EMERGES

SPICER MCNEELEY was the hit of his neighborhood in the summer of 1897. Everyone was talking about Spicer's bicycle—except Beezie Maguire, his former girlfriend. She didn't want to hear anything about it.

Spicer kept his prized possession in the living room of the tenement he shared with his mother. He let the neighborhood young people practice riding in the evenings. Beezie's friends teased her because she was one of the few who hadn't learned to ride.

One afternoon Beezie and her friends went into the McNeeley's empty tenement apartment. They hauled the bicycle up to the rooftop. It was a fairly good place to ride—a flat surface with a bit of a slope. The girls watched as, after a few shaky starts, Beezie rode the bicycle straight into a brick chimney! She wasn't hurt, but the bicycle was badly damaged.

When Spicer heard the news, he stormed across the street to confront Beezie. He demanded to know why Beezie had smashed his bicycle.

"I've a good mind to have you arrested!" he shouted.

Beezie burst into tears.

"Ah, don't do that," Spicer soothed as he threw his arms around his girl.

Later people liked to tell the story about how a bicycle had brought two sweethearts back together in the tenements.

Spicer and Beezie were two people who were enjoying some of the benefits of the Industrial Revolution. The 1800s had introduced new ways of working and living, and as the 1900s dawned, advances in technology, communication, and transportation brought new opportunities for fun and relaxation. Gradually workers began to have a little more free time. Many people began to get Saturday afternoons off from work. That meant they had half of Saturday and all day Sunday to do whatever they wanted. Some employers offered vacation time, although it was usually unpaid.

Advances in manufacturing resulted in many new products for people to buy, such as Spicer's coveted bicycle. Forms of entertainment changed. Hardworking men and women could afford to see the new moving picture shows. People used cameras to record their vacations and fun times. Speedier forms of transportation made it easier for families to travel. Playgrounds and amusement parks were built. Electric lights meant city neighborhoods were safer at night. And residents—such as Spicer and Beezie—were eager to have fun after a hard workweek.

Bicycle daredevil act at an amusement park.

Watching and Playing Sports

THERE WAS a time when sports were meant only for the wealthy. They had money to attend sporting events. They had time to play games. Working people had little of either—money or free time. Over the years of the Industrial Revolution, that changed.

As the 1800s drew to a close, parks, playgrounds, and gymnasiums offered places for working families to participate in sports. Settlement houses and organizations such as the Young Men's Christian Association (YMCA) designed gymnasiums. They were available for use by the public. Stadiums were built where people came to watch sporting events. During the Industrial Revolution, Americans became avid sports watchers and players.

In the early 1880s roller skating was a craze. There were roller skating clubs and races. People liked to watch roller skating races, but they also liked to skate themselves. Empty warehouses were used for skating rinks. Canoeing, ice skating, walking, bowling, golfing, sleighing, and fishing were popular sports also. Americans loved to watch horse racing and canoeing matches. They also watched and played tennis. Baseball, football, and basketball were new sports developed in the United States during the years of the Industrial Revolution.

Organized baseball had its beginnings in the 1840s and '50s. By the late 1800s Americans were wild about this sport. They were delighted with players such as Peter "the Gladiator" Browning, who excelled despite being nearly deaf, and Michael "King" Kelly, famous for stealing bases. Fans shouted, "Slide, Kelly, slide!" every time he rounded the bases. John Montgomery Ward was a well-educated player—he had a law degree—but baseball fans were captivated by his skills on the diamond as a pitcher and shortstop. Catcher Moses Fleetwood Walker was an African American catcher; while some spectators were supportive, others taunted him with racial slurs.

There were multiple professional baseball leagues: the American League, National

Boys playing in city dump in Boston in 1909. It was filled in and converted into a playground.

Courtesy of the National Archives Research Administration, National Child Labor Committee Photographs, ARC Identifier 523225

Roller skating became a popular sport during the Industrial Revolution.

Courtesy of the Library of Congress, Prints & Photographs Division, LC-USZ62-55467

103

WOMEN EXCEL IN TENNIS

Tennis was a popular sport for women. There were many successful female tennis players in the late 1800s and early 1900s. Bessie Moore was the first woman to win the US Women's Singles Championship four times—in 1896, 1901, 1903, and 1905. She was a marvel because she could play equally well with her left or right hand. Grace Roosevelt was described as "one of the best lady players in America" in 1889. Her sister was a champ also. In 1890 Ellen Roosevelt won the US Women's Singles Championship. The same year Grace and Ellen Roosevelt teamed up to capture the US Women's Doubles Championship. They were cousins of two future presidents—Theodore and Franklin Roosevelt. Sisters Juliette and Kathleen Atkinson were singles and doubles tennis stars. Twice they faced each other in semifinal play for the singles championship. Juliette won the singles in 1895 and '97. She won five doubles titles in a row—two with Kathleen as her partner.

These and other women were gifted athletes of their day. But newspaper reports frequently mentioned fashion when they wrote about women's sports. The wearing of bloomers became news when reporting about women's basketball and cycling. And in tennis, the topic was underwear! In 1898 a *New York Times* reporter asked tennis sensation Juliette Atkinson about her underwear. She replied, "The more simply a player can dress on a tennis court, the better. Lace trimmed underclothes should never be worn. The skirts will fly, the lace is conspicuous, and it is not quite nice to wear it."

In the late 1800s women participated in many sports, but their clothes often drew more attention than their athletic skills.

Courtesy of the Library of Congress, Prints & Photographs Division, LC-USZ62-83510

League, Players League, Union Association, and American Association. The Union Association existed only for one year—1884. There were teams representing a variety of cities: Boston Red Stockings, Cincinnati Porkers, Boston Beaneaters, Cleveland Spiders, Brooklyn Bridegrooms, Cleveland Infants, and the Chicago White Stockings.

Football started as a college sport in 1879. Universities such as Princeton, Yale, and Harvard sponsored football teams. There was controversy surrounding the early days of college football. Some thought students spent too much time and attention on football and not enough on class work. Many thought it was a dangerous game that should be eliminated from colleges.

A committee was formed in 1894 to study college football. Representatives from Princeton, Harvard, Yale, and other colleges met to consider changes in game rules. The group hoped to develop a standard set of rules for all colleges across the country. The elimination of the *flying wedge*—rough tackling after a punt—would be under discussion, along with other tactics that were "dangerous to life and limb."

In 1897 an 18-year-old University of Georgia fullback, Richard Von Gammon, suffered a head injury during a game and died. His death spurred the Georgia state legislature to pass a law banning football at the university, but the governor vetoed the bill. He had gotten a letter from Richard's mother asking him not to sign the new law. She said her son lived for football, and he would not want it eliminated from the university.

Professional football was just starting during the Industrial Revolution. Some cities had athletic associations—or clubs—that offered a variety of sports. The Allegheny Athletic Association (AAA), East End Gymnasium Club in Pittsburgh, and the Chicago Athletic Association were established in the 1890s and had football teams. They are considered to be the beginnings of professional football. (It wasn't until 1920 that the American Professional Football Association was formed. In 1922 it changed its name to the National Football League.)

William "Pudge" Heffelfinger was the first player to receive a salary for playing football. He played for a city club, the AAA in Allegheny, Pennsylvania. In 1892 he was paid $500 to play in a game against another city club, the Pittsburgh Athletic Club (PAC). The AAA won, and Pudge became a star when he ran 35 yards for a touchdown.

James Naismith taught physical education at the Springfield, Massachusetts, YMCA in the late 1800s. He was trying to find an indoor sport that could keep athletes in shape between fall football and summer baseball

Americans loved to take a break from work during the Industrial Revolution and watch a game of baseball. Here the New York Giants play the Pittsburgh Pirates in 1908.

Courtesy of the Library of Congress, Prints & Photographs Division, LC-USZ62-97877

seasons. In 1891 he came up with an idea—basketball. He developed 13 rules, borrowed a soccer ball, found some peach buckets to use as hoops, and the rest is history.

Cycling became a very popular sport during the late 1800s. By then bicycles had been around for a while, but their use grew as their design improved. In 1885 there were 400 bicycle factories in the United States. And in 1895

Play "Monkey Tag"

KIDS PLAYED many different versions of tag during the 1800s. One popular form was "Monkey Tag." It's a great game to play after a slow day—like after an afternoon of "screen time" in the 21st century! Get a group of friends together and try it. (This activity is adapted from a game described in a book from 1896, *The American Boy's Book of Sport: Outdoor Games for All Seasons*.)

YOU'LL NEED

➤ A few friends

➤ A large, open space with boundaries marked (a bigger space makes the game more fun and more challenging)

➤ Objects to serve as "bases" (be creative when finding objects to use for bases: hula hoops, baseball bases, trash cans)

Choose one person as "It." The other players are all monkeys. The job of "It" is to capture a monkey by tagging him or her.

Place the bases at random spots in the area, within the boundaries. There must be one fewer base than there are monkeys. For example, if there are 10 monkeys, there should be 9 bases.

Monkeys should make constant screeching sounds to distract "It." Monkeys should keep running from branch to branch. (The bases are called branches because they represent branches of trees.) Monkeys may not stop at any time or for any reason between branches. And they must stay within the boundaries. While on a branch, they continue to jump up and down and make screeching monkey sounds.

"It" tries to tag a monkey between branches. The branches are "safe" places—"It" can't tag the monkeys while they're on a branch. However, no two monkeys can be on the same branch at the same time, so as a second monkey approaches a branch the first monkey must move off and resume running between branches.

When a monkey is tagged, he or she becomes "It," and the original "It" rejoins the game as a monkey. The game is played until all the monkeys are exhausted!

one in every 27 Americans owned a bicycle. There were cycling clubs. And racing was the rage—both doing it and watching it.

As bicycle racing grew in popularity, many talented athletes shone. But one stood out from the others in 1899. Marshall Walter Taylor became known as the "Black Cyclone" in his home state of Indiana. But when he started winning races, he was banned from competition—because he was African American. At a time when racism was openly practiced, a black star athlete was not acceptable in some places.

Marshall moved to Massachusetts, where he began training and had more opportunities to race professionally. His first competition was in New York City in 1896. He traveled all over the world competing in races and set records everywhere he went. In 1899 he won the world one-mile track cycling championship.

Cycling was a pastime that many women enjoyed too. But fashion controversy surrounded women in this sport too, as it did in tennis. At the time, women wore long skirts made with yards of fabric. That made bicycling very awkward. Bloomers or split skirts made cycling much easier. But bloomers and women on bicycles were considered scandalous by some. Even medical experts weighed in. At a medical conference in 1895, male doctors encouraged cycling for men and women.

It was good exercise, they said. But they called bloomers "outrageous."

Reading Leads to Adventure

As the printing process and print materials became more affordable throughout the Industrial Revolution, more people purchased books, magazines, and newspapers. Also, public libraries were open to more people. Andrew Carnegie, the man who had made a fortune in the steel industry, was partly responsible for the availability of libraries. He donated millions of dollars for the construction of libraries in communities all across the country. Between 1886 and 1919 over 1,600 libraries were built with Carnegie funds.

Mark Twain, whose real name was Samuel Clemens, was a beloved author who wrote humorous stories about everyday people. Some of his plots were based on his own adventures. Although his tales were funny and outrageous, they had a serious message—often about racism in America. He is considered a master storyteller. Two of his most popular novels are *The Adventures of Tom Sawyer* and *The Adventures of Huckleberry Finn.*

Marshall Taylor overcame racial discrimination to become a world-famous cyclist.

Courtesy of E. A. Miller and the Major Taylor Association, Inc.

Investigate the Science of Bicycling

EARLY BICYCLES were simple machines. Today's bikes can be more complicated, with multiple gears or speeds. How do the various speeds affect the workings of a bike?

YOU'LL NEED
- Multispeed bike
- Masking tape

Put the bike in the lowest speed. Turn the bike upside down, resting it on the handlebars and seat. You may need to ask a friend to help steady it while you conduct the experiment.

Use masking tape to mark a spot on the back tire. While watching the wheel, turn the pedal one full turn. How many turns does the wheel make for each turn of the pedal?

Turn the bike back to an upright position so you can shift into the highest speed. Flip it upside down again. While watching the tape on the wheel, turn the pedal one full turn. How many turns does the wheel make this time?

You will discover that the wheel will make many more turns when the bike is in the highest speed position. That's why it's more difficult—and more exercise—to pedal in a high gear than in a low gear.

The discovery of gold in Canada near the Klondike River in the late 1890s inspired two popular books. In 1899 Mary Hitchcock wrote about her travels with a friend to the gold fields. Her diary, *Two Women in the Klondike*, introduced readers to the people and places they encountered. It was a bit shocking to readers in a time when women were not encouraged to travel alone—especially to a rough-and-tumble place like the wilds of northern Canada.

Jack London entertained readers in the early 1900s with his adventure stories. They often reflected episodes in his life. One of his most loved novels was *Call of the Wild*, set in the Klondike. The main character was a dog named Buck.

Children's literature was a booming business during the Industrial Revolution. Many of the plots and characters were reflections of real events and people during the time. Orphans, foster families, and working children were subjects of popular kids' books. Some were pure fantasy.

Girls read Rebecca Sophia Clarke's book series about mischievous little kids with names like Little Prudy, Dotty Dimple, and Flaxie Frizzle. The Katy books by Sarah Chauncey Woolsey were also hits. *What Katy Did*, *What Katy Did at School*, and *What Katy Did Next* followed the adventures of Katy Carr, who was a naughty little girl but changed her ways as she recovered from a serious injury. The Elsie series by Martha Finley was the rage between 1867 and 1905. The books featured main character Elsie Dinsmore and followed her from childhood to adulthood.

Boys were reading *Toby Tyler* by James Otis, about a boy who ran away from his foster home to work in a circus. He befriended a chimpanzee named Mr. Stubbs. Also, Dinah Craik's *The Little Lame Prince* captured the imaginations of boys. It was about a paralyzed prince who was able to go on remarkable adventures after he received a magical cloak.

In addition to books, adult readers found magazines to be affordable ways to learn about the world beyond their neighborhoods. *Scribner's Magazine* launched in 1886. It was published monthly and was known for its beautiful color illustrations. *Puck* was a magazine that featured political articles and was known for its political cartoons. They poked fun at well-known people of the time—presidents, politicians, and businessmen.

Popular magazines for women during the Industrial Revolution were *Ladies' Home Journal*, *Woman's Home Companion*, and *Woman's Work*. They all offered articles about home, travel, and health. *Woman's Work* was different than most women's magazines. It was "A Journal Devoted to the Employment of Women." Articles highlighted women's work outside the home, which was unusual for the time. The "Personal" section identified women of interest: "Dr. Mary McLean has been appointed by the St. Louis Board of Health assistant physician at the Women's Hospital." "Mrs. J.D. Hutchins of Springfield, Massachusetts, is one of the most successful business women in the country. She is a dealer in musical instruments."

Newspapers were affordable and accessible to the average citizen. For a penny, readers could get a copy of the daily paper. Some papers published a morning and evening edition. They were packed with world, national, and local news.

Advertisements attracted readers to the latest products, events, and services. "Children's toys: marbles, sleds, and a mechanical whistling and winking boy"; "For adults: imported glove cases, bags of lizard skin, cigar cases." A dentist made the claim "Teeth positively extracted without pain." One ad mentioned a "high-class" comedy show at the opera house—anyone with 10 cents could get in to see the matinee.

Readers learned about injustices and problems that plagued the cities through their newspapers. Reporters became famous for investigating and reporting on the seamier

Toby Tyler was a beloved children's book character in the late 1800s.

THE COMICS

A floppy-eared street urchin with a bald head and dressed in a bright yellow nightshirt became one of the most popular figures in New York City in 1895. Known as "the yellow kid," this comical little fellow was one of the first comic strip characters in America. He was an Irish kid named Mickey Dugan, and he lived in a tenement neighborhood in New York City. The comic strip story followed Mickey, his dog, and his fellow street urchins as they brawled their way through life in their slum neighborhood. Richard Outcault was the artist who created the yellow kid comic. He used the comic to call attention to problems in the slums. Although he used humor, his message was serious.

Comic strips became very popular with newspaper readers in the late 1800s and early 1900s. They had a special format. The cartoonists used a strip of pictures to introduce readers to a cast of characters they would get to know over time. The strips occurred regularly—weekly or daily. The characters' words were written in balloon shapes over their heads. Because the humorous drawings helped tell the stories, even new immigrants who couldn't read English could enjoy a good laugh over the comics. It was a revolutionary way of entertaining readers, and comic strips became a must-have for newspapers.

side of life. These writers were called *muckrakers.* They uncovered (raked) unpleasant stories (muck) about people and organizations that were causing problems. Ida B. Wells was an African American journalist who made people aware of lynchings of black people. Elizabeth Cochrane, who used the pen name "Nellie Bly," pretended to be insane and spent 10 days undercover in Blackwell's Island In-

sane Asylum in New York. After she got out, she wrote about the most terrifying conditions imaginable. The public was shocked. Politicians responded. Nellie's articles—and later her book, *Ten Days in a Mad-House*—helped to convince officials to provide more money for the care of the mentally ill.

John Spargo described the experiences of young breaker boys in coal mines in his book *The Bitter Cry of Children.* "The gloom of the breaker appalled me ... there was blackness, clouds of deadly dust enfolded everything, the harsh, grinding roar of the machinery and the ceaseless rushing of coal through the chutes filled the ears." The book was published in 1906 and called attention to the condition of children in America at the time. Spargo interviewed people to learn about their lives and published his findings. He wrote about poor mothers and their struggles to feed their children. John Spargo's findings made many readers sad. They were shocked and surprised by what they read.

People who worked in meatpacking plants knew about the filth and grime that existed there. They knew that the food products at the plants were processed in unsanitary conditions. But a writer named Upton Sinclair wanted *all* Americans to realize how horrible the meatpacking plants were. So in 1906 he wrote a book titled *The Jungle* in which he described the horror of the meatpacking industry. Sinclair wrote of "thousands of rats" racing around the piles of meat stored on the floors of the plants. He wrote that the workers ran their hands over the piles of meat and swept off "handfuls of the dried dung of rats." Poison was set out on pieces of bread to kill the rats. When the rats ate the poison and died, workers scooped up the bread, poison, and rat carcasses and tossed it all into the meat that was processed for stores. Although it was a book of fiction, many of the situations Sinclair described in *The Jungle* were based on fact. Readers were disgusted and horrified. The book wasn't pleasant reading, but people were fascinated by it.

Books, magazines, and newspapers opened new worlds to people. They took coal miners to hunt for treasure in faraway gold mines, allowed kids to experience magical worlds, permitted voters to poke fun at their presidents, and exposed comfortable Americans to situations that made them squirm.

Fairs Showcase the World

IT'S NEARLY impossible to image a world without ice cream cones, peanut butter, or cotton candy. These are items that were introduced at *world's fairs*, or international expositions, as they were also known.

During the years of the Industrial Revolution the world eagerly awaited these spectacular events, which captured the attention of wealthy entrepreneurs, middle-class families, and factory workers living in slums. The wealthy attended in person; the less fortunate dreamed about the marvels they saw pictured in newspapers and magazines.

The world's fairs took place every few years at a different location. Cities around the world wanted to host the fair. A world's fair was good for the local economy. Ordinary workers such as carpenters, craftsmen, and landscapers got jobs preparing the fairgrounds for the six-month celebration. They put up elaborate buildings designed by architects to show new building techniques. They planted lawns and gardens. Workers built fences and gates, walkways, lakes, and fountains, and even roads in preparation for the big events.

The fairs brought together ideas, inventions, and creative people in one location. Artists, inventors, architects, and engineers showed their creations. Famous people and newcomers wanted to have their work represented. Visitors couldn't wait to get inside the hundreds of acres of fairgrounds to see the latest and greatest new ideas that these geniuses had brought to reality.

Often the fair honored an event in history. The name of the fair reflected the special theme. And each gave the host city and country a chance to show off its industries, arts, and new technologies. The fairs had an international flavor—nations all over the globe were represented through exhibits and events that showcased their cultures.

The American Centennial Exhibition, held in Philadelphia in 1876, celebrated the 100th birthday of the United States. It was the first world's fair held in the United States. Many fairgoers saw a telephone for the first time. They witnessed the miracle of the telegraph that sent messages thousands of miles across the country. Typewriters, electric lights, and elevators were new marvels featured at the fair.

A centerpiece of the Philadelphia fair was a huge steam engine called the Corliss. It was the largest steam engine ever built. The giant engine furnished the power for many of the other machines at the fair.

The United States also hosted the World's Columbian Exposition in 1893. It commemorated Columbus's 1492 voyage to the lands that became North America. There had been a huge debate about which American city would get the fair in 1893. New Yorkers wanted it badly, but Chicago got the fair.

And what a fair it was! For the first time visitors could entertain themselves at an amusement park inside the fairgrounds—complete with a new ride called a Ferris wheel. For 50 cents, riders experienced two complete turns around the 250-foot-diameter wheel. Visitors to the fair drank carbonated drinks and ate hamburgers for the first time.

Electricity was still a new wonder. It dominated the fair and lit the streets at night. Visitors marveled at the electric sidewalk and electric sewing machines, washing machines, and irons. Electric boats carried people around the fairground waterways. Many had heard about—but had never seen—this new source of energy in use.

The Pan-American Exposition of 1901 in Buffalo, New York, had some very big problems. The theme of the fair was peace and progress. But the start of the event was delayed by the Spanish-American War in 1898 and by harsh winter weather. Peace was shattered at the fair by an assassin's gunshot.

President William McKinley visited the fair in September. He was greeting people who were very excited to see the president of the United States. As he reached to shake the hand of Leon Czolgosz, the man unwrapped a gun and shot the president. President McKinley died a few days later, on September 14. Fair officials considered closing the Pan-American Exposition early, but they decided to keep it going. After the president's funeral, the fair reopened.

Design a Product for the World's Fair

THE WORLD'S fairs were eagerly anticipated by people all over the world. They were opportunities for nations to showcase advances in industry, technology, science, and the arts. Inventors competed to show their new products and ideas at the fairs, where hundreds of thousands of visitors from across the globe saw them. The ice cream cone, peanut butter, x-ray machine, and Ferris wheel are just some of the things introduced at world's fairs. And everyone knows how successful they all became.

World's fairs are still held. As in the past, today's fairs give ordinary citizens the opportunity to experience different cultures, innovative technologies, and imaginative inventions. Try your hand at designing a groundbreaking product that could be featured at a world's fair.

The Ferris wheel was introduced at the World's Columbian Exposition in 1893.

Courtesy of the Library of Congress, Prints & Photographs Division, LC-USZ62-50927

YOU'LL NEED
➤ Pencil and paper
➤ Computer with Internet access

Use the following resources to help you get started on brainstorming product ideas:

THE LEMELSON CENTER FOR THE STUDY OF INVENTION AND INNOVATION
http://invention.smithsonian.org/home
This site has resources related to inventions and history. It will give you ideas to help you brainstorm about possible products you can design.

GOOGLE PATENTS
https://www.google.com/?tbm=pts
This site allows you to search patents from the past. Enter any term, such as "action figure," in the search field and look at the results. You will see diagrams and descriptions that have been submitted to the US Patent Office.

PBS DESIGN SQUAD NATION
http://pbskids.org/designsquad
This site provides illustrations and videos of kids designing products. You can get ideas for your design here.

Describe your product. Include the following information:

➤ Name of product (Be creative)
➤ Its purpose
➤ How it works
➤ What it looks like and what it's made of
➤ Why it is groundbreaking—how it is different than anything else out there

Include a detailed diagram or illustration of your product. You can take the design a step further by building a model or the actual product.

One of the most popular exhibits was the US Patent Office section, where visitors could see x-rays revealing their skeletons. Fairgoers also experienced an unusual sensation at the Upside Down House. They entered through the roof. As they climbed the stairs, it appeared they were going down. As they went down, it gave the impression they were going

AN UNFAIR FAIR

Why are not the colored people... who have contributed so large a share to American greatness, more visibly present and better represented in this World's Exposition?

African American writer Ida B. Wells was angry, and she wanted people to know it. The World's Columbian Exposition held in Chicago in 1893 was supposed to celebrate America's progress and greatness. It commemorated Christopher Columbus's arrival in the land that would become America. The fair honored 400 years of history.

Throughout those years, generations of African Americans had contributed greatly to advances in agriculture, industry, music, education, medicine, and other areas of society. Ida and other African American leaders wanted black people to be on the committee that selected groups and individuals who could set up exhibits at the fair. They were denied the privilege. They also asked to be allowed to design an exhibit that would show the advances made

Ida B. Wells used her writing skills to expose injustice.

Courtesy of the Library of Congress, Prints & Photographs Division, LC-USZ62-107756

by African Americans since their arrival in America—first as slaves and then as free men and women. But again, they were denied.

Planners believed they were being generous by proclaiming one day "Negro Day" at the fair. Some black leaders thought it wasn't a bad idea and agreed to participate. But Ida thought Negro Day was an insult. To her it just seemed to reinforce the racist practice of separateness, or segregation, between black and white Americans.

Ida protested by asking three other black leaders to coauthor a pamphlet with her. They wrote "The Reason Why the Colored American Is Not in the World's Columbian Exposition." It outlined the injustices experienced by black Americans at the fair and in society in general. Ida distributed the pamphlet inside the fair. Although she was disappointed that African Americans were not fairly represented at the World's Columbian Exposition, she used her skills as a writer to call attention to injustices that needed to be corrected.

up. When they reached the "top" of the house, they were on the ground floor. It was mind-boggling but fun for the fairgoers.

The Louisiana Purchase Exposition was held in St. Louis, Missouri, in 1904. Visitors strolled 75 miles of roads and walkways. The fairgrounds spread over 1,200 acres. Meteorological balloon experiments, which sent small balloons up to altitudes of 51,000 feet to record temperatures, captured the attention of fairgoers.

The world's fairs celebrated the advances brought about by the Industrial Revolution. There was much to be proud of when it came to innovative technologies and creative ideas. However, the fairs kept alive some of the old ways of thinking too.

Some groups were not represented in ways that respected and honored their traditions and customs. Rather than celebrating the diversity of the world's cultures, sometimes the fair exhibits and shows ridiculed and enforced stereotypes of various peoples. Native Americans were usually portrayed as uncivilized savages who had been tamed by white Americans. People from other cultures were put on display—almost like animals in a zoo. African Americans asked to be part of the planning of exhibits in Chicago and Buffalo, but they were denied. At the Chicago event African Americans were kept from most jobs.

They were limited to positions as waiters and janitors.

Entertainment for the Working Family

Meet Me in St. Louis, Louis
We will dance the Hoochie-Koochie
I will be your Tootsie Wootsie

"MEET ME in St. Louis" was a popular song in 1904. Everybody recognized it, hummed the melody, and thought about going to St. Louis, Missouri, to the world's fair. But many couldn't travel great distances just to attend a fair.

If Americans couldn't make it to a world's fair, there were plenty of other entertainment options for them in the late 1800s and early 1900s. Opera houses were common gathering places for performances. Some had balconies. Sometimes they offered operas, but usually they were used for other types of entertainment—plays, concerts, comedy shows, and vaudeville acts. Many communities—both big cities and small, rural towns—had an opera house. Local groups performed, or traveling shows came to town for a one-night performance.

Vaudeville shows were popular beginning in the 1880s. They included a wide variety of short acts. Jugglers, impersonators, comedians, singers, dancers, magicians, and trained animals might be in a show. Some vaudeville shows went on the road.

Chautauquas were traveling shows of the Industrial Revolution era. But they were more educational than vaudeville shows. They included several days of lectures, plays, and concerts—all meant to improve the mind. They were especially popular in small towns, where residents had fewer opportunities to experience the types of programs offered by the chautauquas. Rural areas offered wide open spaces where the events could be held in large tents or under a grove of trees in the summer.

Entertainment changed drastically when movie houses began to open. In the early 1900s moving picture shows were available for the public. The films were in black and white. There was no sound. Any important dialogue had to be printed on-screen, and a live orchestra in the theater provided musical accompaniment. It wasn't until the 1920s that sound was incorporated into movies. But before that, moviegoers were wild about their silent movies and the stars whom they never heard speak. Charlie Chaplin, Lillian Gish, Tom Mix, Gloria Swanson, and Rudolph Valentino were among the silent-film celebrities of the day.

Advantages of the Industrial Revolution

THE INDUSTRIAL Revolution brought amazing changes to life in America. Throughout the 1800s and into the 1900s people experienced new ways of relaxing and having fun. Revolutionary inventions and ideas made these experiences possible. As Americans learned to adapt to new ways of working and living, they welcomed the advantages that the Industrial Revolution offered.

EPILOGUE

THE INDUSTRIAL REVOLUTION SPANNED ABOUT 100 YEARS. It was a time of vast change in the way people worked, traveled, and communicated. Those changes led to opportunities for people from all levels of society. Creative businesspeople tried new ideas for making money. Dreamers invented awe-inspiring objects. Workers demanded fair wages and safe working conditions. It was also a time of risk taking. Investors put huge sums of money into businesses that could succeed or fail. Inventors gambled life savings on realizing their dreams. Workers jeopardized their jobs to strike for better working conditions for themselves and future generations.

People who study the past recognize the heroes of the Industrial Revolution. They also remember the villains. Who were the heroes? Who were the villains? In some cases, it's easy to answer those questions. The reformers who tried to improve the care of kids and the poor gave hope to many helpless people. The scammers who met newly arrived immigrants as they stepped off the boats were not to be admired.

Who are the heroes of the Industrial Revolution? Wealthy businesspeople like J. D. Rockefeller and Andrew Carnegie? Their companies created jobs for many workers. Their investments in oil and steel gave rise to new industries and products that are still important in today's world. They gave huge sums of money to worthy causes. Thomas Edison, a pioneer in the harnessing of electricity; Alexander Graham Bell, creator of the telephone; and George Eastman, who gave the world the affordable Kodak camera, are honored as great men of the era. They were extremely wealthy as a result of the Industrial Revolution. They are remembered as champions of the industrial age. However, it would be unfair to remember only their heroic actions. At times they showed astonishing disregard for their fellow human beings. They influenced history in both good and bad ways.

Who are the heroes of the Industrial Revolution? What about the men who built the National Road from Cumberland, Maryland, to Vandalia, Illinois, in 1838? What were their names? Was Chief Joseph, leader of the Nez Perce, a hero because he allowed himself to be called by an English name and moved his people out of the way of the Industrial Revolution? Pony Express riders? Most of their names have been forgotten. Young boys who worked as breakers in the coal mines? And 10-year-old girls who toiled in mills? Their faces are captured in photographs and preserved at national museums and libraries. But in most cases, their names were not recorded. How about the women who tried to make homes for their families in dirty, crowded tenement flats after working 14 hours in a factory? Maybe their families appreciated their efforts at the time, but their great-grandchildren didn't see their names in history books. The Chinese immigrants who laid rails across the western United States? Many Americans didn't bother to try pronouncing their unfamiliar names. It was easier to lump them all together as "Chinamen."

The Industrial Revolution produced incredible inventions, introduced groundbreaking technologies, and propelled the world into a time and place that seemed magical. Many ordinary and extraordinary people made it all possible.

RESOURCES

Books to Read

Bancroft, Jessie H. *Games for the Playground, Home, School and Gymnasium.* New York: Macmillan Company, 1909.

Beard, Daniel C. *The American Boy's Book of Sport: Outdoor Games for All Seasons.* New York: Charles Scribner's Sons, 1896.

Beard, Lina, and Adelia B. Beard. *Indoor and Outdoor Handicraft and Recreation for Girls.* New York: Charles Scribner's Sons, 1904.

Larcom, Lucy. *A New England Girlhood Outlined from Memory.* 1889. Available at Project Gutenberg, www.gutenberg.org/files/2293/2293-h/2293-h.htm.

Places to Visit

EDISON AND FORD WINTER ESTATES
2350 McGregor Blvd.
Fort Myers, Florida
www.edisonfordwinterestates.org
VISITORS CAN tour the houses and grounds of the winter homes of Thomas Edison and Henry Ford.

THE HENRY FORD MUSEUM AND GREENFIELD VILLAGE
20900 Oakwood Blvd.
Dearborn, Michigan
www.hfmgv.org
THIS WEBSITE brings to life objects, stories, and lives from the Industrial Revolution through online exhibits and photos. The museum offers visitors a trip into the past with authentic exhibits, historic village and farm sites, a railroad depot, and other captivating experiences, including a ride in a Model T automobile.

NATIONAL POSTAL MUSEUM

2 Massachusetts Ave. NE

Washington, DC

www.postalmuseum.si.edu

THE SMITHSONIAN National Postal Museum is located in a former post office building. Visitors can tour exhibits that tell the story of the postal system and stamp production. Five exhibit galleries house vehicles used for postal transportation, mailboxes and mailbags, uniforms, and equipment.

PONY EXPRESS NATIONAL MUSEUM

914 Penn St.

St. Joseph, Missouri

http://ponyexpress.org

A VISIT to the museum transports visitors to the 1860s, when the Pony Express operated. Exhibits feature a one-room pony school, stables, a blacksmith and leather shop, and an interactive oxen and wagon experience.

TENEMENT MUSEUM

103 Orchard St.

New York, NY

www.tenement.org

THE MUSEUM allows visitors to experience life as an immigrant in New York City in the 19th and early 20th centuries. Inside exhibits recreate life in tenement apartments, businesses, and sweatshops. A walking tour explores the neighborhoods where millions of early immigrants lived, worked, and played. Actors bring the stories to life.

WORLD'S FAIRS

www.worldsfairs.com/Worlds_Fairs
/Calendar_%26_Links.html

WORLD'S FAIRS are held at various places around the world. Fairgoers can attend a fair and learn about innovative ideas and modern inventions—just as early fairgoers did—but with a modern twist. To learn where the next fair will be held, consult this website.

Websites to Explore

AFRICAN AMERICAN PHOTOGRAPHS ASSEMBLED FOR THE 1900 PARIS EXPOSITION

www.loc.gov/pictures/collection/anedub

THIS SITE houses a collection of photographs used in a display for the world's fair in Paris, showing the history and contributions of African Americans.

BASEBALL CARDS

www.loc.gov/pictures/collection/bbc

MORE THAN 2,000 early baseball cards from 1887 to 1914 are presented at this site.

CARTOON DRAWINGS: SWANN COLLECTION OF CARICATURE AND CARTOON

www.loc.gov/pictures/collection/swa

THIS WEBSITE has more than 2,000 drawings, prints, and paintings of cartoons and comic strips.

GEORGE GRANTHAM BAIN COLLECTION

www.loc.gov/pictures/collection/ggbain

THIS COLLECTION includes photographs of sporting events, theater, crime, strikes, disasters, political events, and more from the early 1900s and earlier.

NATIONAL CHILD LABOR COMMITTEE COLLECTION

www.loc.gov/pictures/collection/nclc

THIS SITE contains many of the photographs taken by Lewis Hine while he worked for the National Child Labor Committee documenting children in the workplace between 1908 and 1924.

NATIONAL ORPHAN TRAIN COMPLEX

http://orphantraindepot.org

THIS SITE is dedicated to the preservation of the stories and artifacts of those who were part of the Orphan Train Movement between 1854 and 1929.

NOTES

Introduction

"I thought it would be a pleasure to feel": Larcom, *A New England Girlhood Outlined from Memory*, www.gutenberg.org/files/2293/2293-h/2293-h.htm.

Lucy described it as "miserable": Dulany Addison, *Lucy Larcom: Life, Letters and Diary*, 24.

One day one of her students: Dulany Addison, *Lucy Larcom: Life, Letters and Diary*, 28.

1. A Time of Sweeping Change

People were stunned: National Park Service, "Kingston: Discover 300 Years of New York History," www.nps.gov/nr/travel/kingston/transport.htm.

"There is a great deal of jolting": Dickens, *American Notes for General Circulation*, vol. 1, 146.

During the Second Industrial Revolution... more than 500,000: Sobel et al., *The Challenge of Freedom*, 390.

Between 1860 and 1870, the number of factories: Carman, Syrett, and Wishy, *A History of the American People*, 703.

For example, in 1864, factory workers: Carman, Syrett, and Wishy, *A History of the American People*, 703.

Hardworking miners pried: Zinn, *A People's History of the United States*, 188.

With 193,000 miles of railroad track: Zinn, *A People's History of the United States*, 187.

About 22,000 workers: Zinn, *A People's History of the United States*, 189.

2. New Ways of Working

A minister in Brooklyn, New York, described the situation: "Suicide Is a Coward's Act," *New York Times*, September 17, 1894.

"They are filthy and dishonest": "The Sweat-shop System," *New York Times*, March 9, 1899.

However, in 1899 it was estimated: Fabricant, *The Output of Manufacturing Industries, 1899–1937*, 132.

"We object to them because:" "Address to the People of the State of California and of the United States," *Union Democrat*, July 31, 1869.

3. New Ways of Living

"The place was alive with rats": "Locked Up with the Rats," *New York Times*, April 18, 1893.

Nettie Shea and Eliza Trainor: "Women in Falling Elevator," *New York Times*, August 1, 1899.

In the summer of 1899 well-to-do families: "'Kodak Fiends' at Newport," *New York Times*, August 18, 1899.

In August 1899 the workers: "Drives an Automobile," *New York Times*, August 20, 1899.

4. Kids at Work

Fires raged in the mine: "Will Find Live Miners Waiting," *Lewiston Evening Journal*, November 22, 1909.

As they left the theater: "Hartford Newsboys and Girls Treated," *New York Times*, January 2, 1896.

"Well, my dad was a hard 'un": "The Children's Aid Society," *New York Times*, December 22, 1860.

"I am doing all": Library of Congress, "The Oblinger Family and Their Letters," http://memory.loc.gov/cgi-bin/query/r?ammem/ps:@field(DOCID+L188).

"I must tell you about Prince": Library of Congress, "The Oblinger Family and Their Letters," http://memory.loc.gov/cgi-bin/query/r?ammem/ps:@field(DOCID+L327).

"I always go": Library of Congress, "The Oblinger Family and Their Letters," http://memory.loc.gov/cgi-bin/query/r?ammem/ps:@field(DOCID+L325).

"It is worse than futile to assume": US Bureau of Education, *Report of the Commissioner of Education for the Year 1888–89*, vol. 1, 526.

They earned job promotions: "School for Store Children," *New York Times*, November 10, 1901.

5. Catastrophes, Unions, and Strikes

"deafening thunders": "Eleven Lives Lost," *New York Times*, February 26, 1889.

"death-like pall": "Eleven Lives Lost," *New York Times*, February 26, 1889.

Finally, in 1837 the city: Explore PA History, "Mechanics' Union of Trade Associations Historical Marker," http://explorepahistory.com/hmarker.php?markerId=1-A-BC.

"the task of asserting": US Bureau of Labor, *Report on the Condition of Woman and Child Wage-Earners*, vol. 9, 81.

"I don't care what you do": Frost-Knappman and Cullen-DuPont, *Women's Suffrage in America*, 31.

"If we worked only 11 hours": "Strike Among the Operatives at Lewiston," *New York Times*, April 10, 1854.

Our Bosses Grind Us: "The Bay State Strike," *New York Times*, February 29, 1860.

"It reminds me of a seething volcano": "Trouble Bound to Come," *New York Times*, July 30, 1892.

6. Help and Hope for Better Lives

"They spank us": "Spankings and Prayers Cause Another Outbreak in the Howard Orphan Asylum," *Brooklyn Daily Eagle*, April 8, 1895.

At the time there were an estimated 100,000: Keiger, "The Rise and Demise of the American Orphanage," *Johns Hopkins Magazine*, www.jhu.edu/jhumag/496web/orphange.html.

"Do you want to go where": "These Boys Very Tired of Home," *New York Times*, February 13, 1894.

Rowdy kids were locked away: "Cruelty in a House of Refuge," *New York Times*, February 7, 1884.

Over the next 22 years: American Society for the Prevention of Cruelty to Animals, "About Us," www.aspca.org/about-us/history.aspx

The number grew to 2 million: National Archives, "Photographs of Lewis Hine: Documentation of Child Labor," www.archives.gov/education/lessons/hine-photos.

Three million workers: Danzer et al., *The Americans*, 397.

"men and women who would die": "The Nineteenth Ward Relief Committee," *New York Times*, February 1, 1874.

By the end of that year, over 15,000: Danzer et al., *The Americans*, 427.

"It has seemed to us": Recchiuti, *Civic Engagement: Social Science and Progressive-Era Reform in New York City*, 68.

"the angel of the tenements": "Angel of the Tenements," *New York Times*, April 27, 1902.

At one point the number rose: *Encyclopedia of Chicago*, "Settlement Houses," www.encyclopedia.chicagohistory.org/pages/1135.html.

7. A New Culture Emerges

"The more simply a player can dress": "A Girl Tennis Champion," *New York Times*, July 10, 1898.

The elimination of the *flying wedge*: "Consistent Rules Nationwide," *New York Times*, February 4, 1894.

And in 1895 one in every 27: Exploratorium, "Science of Cycling," www.exploratorium.edu/cycling/wheel2.html.

At a medical conference in 1895, male doctors: "Bloomers Abhorred," *Iowa State Register*, September 7, 1895.

Between 1886 and 1919: National Park Service, "Carnegie Libraries: The Future Made Bright," www.nps.gov/nr/twhp/wwwlps/lessons/50carnegie/50carnegie.htm.

BIBLIOGRAPHY

Books

Bancroft, Jessie H. *Games for the Playground, Home, School and Gymnasium.* New York: Macmillan Company, 1909.

Beard, Daniel C. *The American Boy's Book of Sport: Outdoor Games for All Seasons.* New York: Charles Scribner's Sons, 1896.

Beard, Lina, and Adelia B. Beard. *Indoor and Outdoor Handicraft and Recreation for Girls.* New York: Charles Scribner's Sons, 1904.

Burfeind, James, and Dawn Bartusch. *Juvenile Delinquency: An Integrated Approach.* Sudbury, MA: Jones & Bartlett Publishers, 2005.

Burstyn, Joan N. *Past and Promise: Lives of New Jersey Women.* Scarecrow Press, 1990.

Carman, H., H. Syrett, and B. Wishy. *A History of the American People.* New York: Alfred A. Knopf, 1967.

Danzer, G., J. Klor de Alva, L. Krieger, L. Wilson, and N. Woloch. *The Americans.* Orlando, FL: Houghton Mifflin Harcourt, 2012.

Degler, Carl N. *Out of Our Past.* 3rd ed. New York: Harper & Row, 1983.

Dickens, Charles. *American Notes for General Circulation.* Vol. 1. London: Chapman and Hall, 1842.

Dulany Addison, Daniel. *Lucy Larcom: Life, Letters and Diary.* New York: Houghton Mifflin, 1895.

Fabricant, Solomon. *The Output of Manufacturing Industries, 1899–1937.* New York: National Bureau of Economic Research, 1940.

Foner, Philip S., and Robert J. Branham, eds. *Lift Every Voice: African American Oratory, 1787–1900.* Tuscaloosa: University of Alabama Press, 1998.

Frost-Knappman, Elizabeth, and Kathryn Cullen-DuPont. *Women's Suffrage in America.* Updated ed. New York: Facts on File, 2005.

Larcom, Lucy. *A New England Girlhood Outlined from Memory.* 1889. Available at Project Gutenberg, www.gutenberg.org/files/2293/2293-h/2293-h.htm.

McNichol, Tom. *AC/DC: The Savage Tale of the First Standards War.* John Wiley & Sons, 2006.

Recchiuti, John Louis. *Civic Engagement: Social Science and Progressive-Era Reform in New York City.* Philadelphia: University of Pennsylvania Press, 2007.

Sicherman, Barbara, and Carol Hurd Green, eds. *Notable American Women: A Biographical Dictionary.* Vol. 4, *The Modern Period.* Belknap Press of Harvard University Press, 1986.

Sobel, R., R. LaRaus, L. De Leon, and H. Morris. *The Challenge of Freedom.* River Forest, IL: Laidlaw Brothers, 1982.

Zinn, Howard. *A People's History of the United States.* Abridged teaching ed. New York: New Press, 2003.

Journals

Fox, Sanford. "Juvenile Justice Reform: An Historical Perspective." *Stanford Law Review* 22, no. 6 (June 1970): 1187–1239.

Thomas, Bettye C. "A Nineteenth Century Black Operated Shipyard, 1866–1884: Reflections upon Its Inception and Ownership," *Journal of Negro History* 59, no. 1 (January 1974).

Magazines

Keiger, Dale. "The Rise and Demise of the American Orphanage," *Johns Hopkins Magazine,* April 1996. www.jhu.edu /jhumag/496web/orphange.html.

"The St. Andrew Coffee-House Charity," *Frank Leslie's Sunday Magazine* 21 (January–June 1887).

Newspapers

Brooklyn Daily Eagle. "Spankings and Prayers Cause Another Outbreak in the Howard Orphan Asylum." April 8, 1895.

Iowa State Register. "Bloomers Abhorred." September 7, 1895.

Lewiston Evening Journal. "Will Find Live Miners Waiting." November, 22, 1909.

Milwaukee Journal. "Death in Football Game." November 1, 1897.

New York Times. "Angel of the Tenements." April 27, 1902.

New York Times. "The Bay State Strike. Movement Among the Women, Acts and Proceedings of Employers and Workers." February 29, 1860.

New York Times. "Chased by 300 Factory Girls." May 14, 1895.

New York Times. "The Children's Aid Society." December 22, 1860.

New York Times. "Coney Elephant Killed." January 5, 1903.

New York Times. "Consistent Rules Nationwide." February 4, 1894.

New York Times. "Cruelty in a House of Refuge." February 7, 1884.

New York Times. "Drives an Automobile." August 20, 1899.

New York Times. "Eleven Lives Lost." February 26, 1889.

New York Times. "A Girl Tennis Champion." July 10, 1898.

New York Times. "Hartford Newsboys and Girls Treated." January 2, 1896.

New York Times. "'Kodak Fiends' at Newport." August 18, 1899.

New York Times. "Locked Up with the Rats." April 18, 1893.

New York Times. "The Nineteenth Ward Relief Committee." February 1, 1874.

New York Times. "Report on Meat Converts Cannon." May 28, 1906.

New York Times. "School for Store Children." November 10, 1901.

New York Times. "Spicer McNeeley's Wheel." August 30, 1895.

New York Times. "Strike Among the Operatives at Lewiston—Speech of a Factory Girl." April 10, 1854.

New York Times. "Suicide Is a Coward's Act." September 17, 1894.

New York Times. "The Sweatshop System." March 9, 1899.

New York Times. "Trouble Bound to Come." July 30, 1892.

New York Times. "Teachers Guarded by Officers." September 7, 1892.

New York Times. "These Boys Very Tired of Home." February 13, 1894.

New York Times. "Women in Falling Elevator." August 1, 1899.

Owosso American. "Great Railroad Strike." July 25, 1877.

Union Democrat. "Address to the People of the State of California and of the United States." July 31, 1869.

Reports

US Bureau of Education. *Report of the Commissioner of Education for the Year 1888–89.* Vol. 1. Washington, DC: Government Printing Office, 1891. Available at Google Books, http://books.google.com/books?id=R680 AQAAMAAJ.

US Bureau of Labor. *Report on the Condition of Woman and Child Wage-Earners in the United States.* Vol. 9, *History of Women in Industry in the United States.* Washington, DC: Government Printing Office, 1910. Available at Google Books, http://books.google.com /books?id=3w0wAAAAYAAJ.

Websites

American Humane Association. "Mary Ellen Wilson." www.americanhumane.org/about -us/who-we-are/history/mary-ellen-wilson .html.

American Society for the Prevention of Cruelty to Animals. "About Us." www.aspca.org /about-us/history.aspx.

Encyclopedia of Chicago. "Settlement Houses." www.encyclopedia.chicagohistory.org/pages /1135.html.

Exploratorium. "Science of Cycling." www .exploratorium.edu/cycling/wheel2.html.

Explore PA History. "Mechanics' Union of Trade Associations Historical Marker." http:// explorepahistory.com/hmarker.php?marker Id=1-A-BC.

The J. Paul Getty Museum. "Lewis Wickes Hine." www.getty.edu/art/gettyguide/art MakerDetails?maker=1601.

Library of Congress. "The Oblinger Family and Their Letters." American Memory, Prairie Settlement, Nebraska Photographs and Family Letters, 1862–1912. http://memory.loc .gov/ammem/award98/nbhihtml/pshome .html.

Library of Congress. "Owney, the Railway Mail Dog." Topics in Chronicling America. www.loc.gov/rr/news/topics/owney.html.

National Archives. "Photographs of Lewis Hine: Documentation of Child Labor." Teaching with Documents. www.archives .gov/education/lessons/hine-photos.

National Park Service. "Kingston: Discover 300 Years of New York History." www.nps .gov/nr/travel/kingston/transport.htm.

National Park Service. "Carnegie Libraries: The Future Made Bright." Teaching with Historic Places. www.nps.gov/nr/twhp/wwwlps /lessons/50carnegie/50carnegie.htm.

INDEX

Page numbers in *italics* indicate pictures